P9-DBI-467

Taste of Home's

Pasta cookbook

LOOKING for family-friendly fare that works well with your hurried, hectic weekdays? In the time it takes to boil water, you can turn the pages of *Taste of Home's Pasta Cookbook* and come up with 178 pleasing "pastabilities"!

Put a tasty twist on linguine with Vegetarian Linguine (pictured above). For out-of-the-ordinary lasagna, dish out Pepperoni Lasagna, Spinach Lasagna Roll-Ups or Lasagna Con Carne.

Mouth-watering manicotti (like Cheesy Chicken Manicotti on page 47) adds spark to every-day dinners. And for fare that will always satisfy, rely on such classics as Italian Pasta [illegible] Hearty Chicken Noodle Soup, Fettuccine Alfredo and Turkey Tetrazzini.

So when your famished family asks, "What's for dinner?", use your noodle and re[illegible] of *Taste of Home's Pasta Cookbook*!

641.822
TAS

p. 6
p. 1
p. 38
p. 5
p. 74
p. 8

p. 28

p. 62

p. 98

Contents

Editor: Jean Steiner
Senior Book Editor: Julie Schnittka
Art Director: Catherine Fletcher
Executive Editor/Books: Heidi Reuter Lloyd
Proofreader: Julie Blume Benedict
Editorial Assistant: Barb Czysz
Food Editor: Janaan Cunningham
Associate Food Editors: Coleen Martin, Diane Werner
Senior Recipe Editor: Sue A. Jurack
Recipe Editors: Janet Briggs, Mary King
Food Photography: Rob Hagen, Dan Roberts, Jim Wieland
Set Stylists: Julie Ferron, Stephanie Marchese,
Sue Myers, Jennifer Bradley Vent
Food Stylists: Kristin Arnett, Sarah Thompson, Joylyn Trickel
Photographers Assistant: Lori Foy
Senior Vice President/Editor in Chief: Catherine Cassidy
President: Barbara Newton
Chairman and Founder: Roy Reiman

Taste of Home's Pasta Cookbook

©2005 Reiman Media Group, Inc.
5400 S. 60th St., Greendale WI 53129
International Standard Book Number: 0-89821-468-8
Library of Congress Control Number: 2005935297
All rights reserved.
Printed in U.S.A.

There's a world of "pastabilities" when it comes to making dishes your family will love. Staples like spaghetti with meat sauce, fettuccine Alfredo and lasagna are proven crowd-pleasers.

But the number of pasta options at the supermarket is enough to make even the savviest shopper's head spin. There are dozens of pastas available ...all in different shapes, sizes, tastes and textures.

For the most part, busy cooks can rely on fast-to-cook dry pastas. See the photos at right for a few of the most common shapes.

Spaghetti, linguine, angel hair, vermicelli and egg noodles are no-fuss pastas that suit a variety of recipes.

Bow tie and rotini offer a bit of fun but still cook up quickly.

Medium shells and tubular pastas, like elbow macaroni and mostaccioli, are wonderful in cold salads...and jumbo shells and manicotti are best suited for stuffing with savory fillings.

Now that you know more about these common pasta shapes, why not try them out in any of the recipes that follow? Your family will soon be asking for "More pasta, please!"

Angel Hair

Bow Tie

Fettuccine

Lasagna

Rotini (Spiral)

Shells, Jumbo

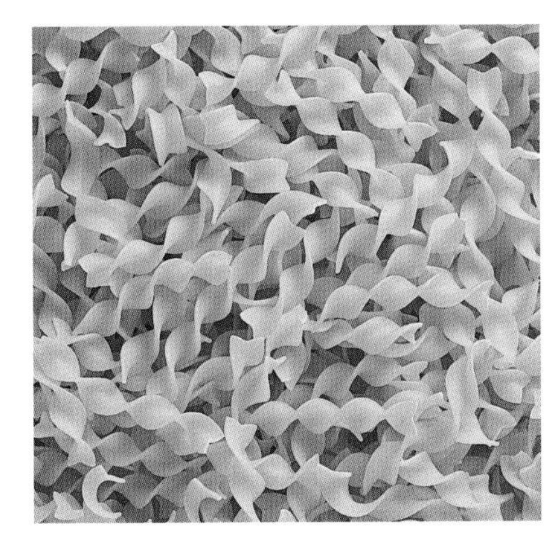
Egg Noodles, Medium

Egg Noodles, Wide

Elbow Macaroni

Linguine

Manicotti

Mostaccioli

Shells, Medium

Spaghetti

Vermicelli

Soups

Turkey Minestrone (p. 14)

Too-Easy Tortellini Soup

(Pictured above)

Beth Daley, Chesterfield, Missouri

I combine packaged tortellini and canned goods to quickly bring this hearty soup to the table. Basil and Parmesan cheese round out the flavor of this family favorite.

4 cups chicken broth
1 package (9 ounces) refrigerated cheese tortellini
1 can (15 ounces) white kidney *or* cannellini beans, rinsed and drained
1 can (14-1/2 ounces) Italian diced tomatoes, undrained
1-1/2 teaspoons dried basil
1 tablespoon red wine vinegar
Shredded Parmesan cheese and coarsely ground pepper, optional

In a large saucepan, bring broth to a boil. Stir in tortellini. Reduce heat; simmer, uncovered, for 4 minutes, stirring occasionally. Stir in the beans, tomatoes and basil. Simmer for 4-6 minutes or until pasta is tender. Stir in the vinegar. Sprinkle with Parmesan cheese and pepper if desired. **Yield:** 6 servings.

Potluck Pasta Soup

Marilyn Foss, Beavertown, Ohio

In an attempt to duplicate a soup served at an Italian restaurant, I came up with this recipe. Friends and family are willing dinner guests when it's on the menu.

1-1/2 pounds ground beef
2 quarts water
2 cans (14-1/2 ounces *each*) Italian stewed tomatoes
2 cups diced carrots
1-1/2 cups diced celery
1 cup chopped onion
1 can (8 ounces) tomato sauce
1 envelope onion soup mix
1 tablespoon sugar
1 teaspoon Italian seasoning
2 garlic cloves, minced
2 bay leaves
1/2 teaspoon pepper
3 cups cooked elbow macaroni
1 can (15 ounces) garbanzo beans, rinsed and drained
1/2 cup chopped green pepper

In a soup kettle or Dutch oven, cook beef over medium heat until no longer pink; drain. Add water, tomatoes, carrots, celery, onion, tomato sauce, soup mix, sugar and seasonings; bring to a boil.

Reduce heat; simmer, uncovered, for 1 hour. Stir in macaroni, beans and green pepper; heat through. Discard bay leaves before serving. **Yield:** 20 servings (5 quarts).

Pasta Pizza Soup

Linda Fox, Soldotna, Alaska

This soup has a pleasant combination of tender vegetables, pasta spirals and ground beef.

1 pound ground beef
4 ounces fresh mushrooms, sliced
1 medium onion, chopped
1 celery rib, thinly sliced
1 garlic clove, minced
4 cups water
1 can (14-1/2 ounces) Italian diced tomatoes, undrained
2 medium carrots, chopped
4 teaspoons beef bouillon granules
1 bay leaf
1-1/2 teaspoons dried oregano
1-1/2 cups cooked tricolor spiral pasta

In a large saucepan over medium heat, cook beef, mushrooms, onion, celery and garlic until meat is no longer pink and vegetables are tender; drain. Stir in water, tomatoes, carrots, bouillon, bay leaf and oregano. Bring to a boil.

Reduce heat; cover and simmer for 20-25 minutes or until carrots are tender. Stir in pasta; heat through. Discard bay leaf. **Yield:** 8 servings (about 2 quarts).

Chicken Soup With Stuffed Noodles

(Pictured at right)

Jennifer Bucholtz, Kitchener, Ontario

Before retiring, I worked as a cook for 15 years. Now I spend lots of time in my kitchen preparing new, interesting food for my family. You'll love this rich homey soup.

1 broiler-fryer chicken (3 to 3-1/2 pounds), cut up
2-1/2 quarts water
2 teaspoons salt
1/4 teaspoon pepper
4 medium carrots, sliced
2 celery ribs, sliced
1 medium onion, diced

NOODLES:

1-1/4 cups all-purpose flour
1 teaspoon salt
1 egg
5 tablespoons water
1 teaspoon vegetable oil

FILLING:

2 eggs
1-1/4 cups seasoned bread crumbs
3 tablespoons butter, melted

Place chicken, water, salt and pepper in a large soup kettle. Cover and bring to a boil; skim fat. Reduce heat; cover and simmer 1-1/2 hours or until chicken is tender. Remove chicken; allow to cool. Add vegetables to broth; cook until tender. Debone chicken and cut into chunks; return to broth.

Meanwhile, for noodles, mix flour and salt in a medium bowl. Make a well in the center. Beat together the egg, water and oil; pour into well. Stir together, forming a dough. Turn dough onto a floured surface; knead 8-10 times. Roll into a 16-in. x 12-in. rectangle.

Combine filling ingredients; mix well. Sprinkle over dough to within 1/2 in. of edge; pat down. Moisten edges with water. Roll up jelly-roll style from long end; cut into 1/2-in. slices. Add noodles to gently boiling soup and cook for 6-8 minutes or until tender. **Yield:** 10 servings (2-1/2 quarts).

Oodles of Noodles Soup

(Pictured below)

Lorri Reinhardt, Big Bend, Wisconsin

I often gave my godchild a children's cookbook for her birthday or other special occasions. We'd plan an entire menu from the books, prepare the meal together and serve it to her family. This soup recipe was a favorite.

3/4 pound boneless skinless chicken breasts, cubed
2 medium carrots, sliced
1 small onion, chopped
2 celery ribs, sliced
1 garlic clove, minced
5 cups water
1/4 teaspoon pepper
2 packages (3 ounces *each*) chicken ramen noodles

In a large saucepan coated with nonstick cooking spray, saute the chicken, carrots, onion, celery and garlic until chicken is no longer pink. Add water, pepper and contents of seasoning packets from the noodles. Bring to a boil. Reduce heat; cover and simmer for 15-20 minutes or until carrots are tender.

Break noodles into pieces and add to soup; cover and cook for 3 minutes or until tender. **Yield:** 6 servings.

Turkey Noodle Soup

Elaine Bickford, Las Vegas, Nevada

Homemade taste makes this chunky soup a favorite of mine. We enjoy it with hot bread in winter and with salad in summer.

2 cans (14-1/2 ounces *each*) chicken broth
3 cups water
1-3/4 cups sliced carrots
1/2 cup chopped onion
2 celery ribs, sliced
1 package (12 ounces) frozen egg noodles
3 cups chopped cooked turkey
1 package (10 ounces) frozen peas
2 envelopes chicken gravy mix
1/2 cup cold water

In a large saucepan, bring the broth, water, carrots, onion and celery to a boil. Reduce heat; cover and simmer for 4-6 minutes or until vegetables are crisp-tender. Add the noodles. Simmer, uncovered, for 20 minutes or until noodles are tender.

Stir in turkey and peas. Combine gravy mixes and cold water until smooth; stir into the soup. Bring to a boil; cook and stir for 2 minutes or until thickened. **Yield:** 7 servings.

Pasta Meatball Soup

Beverly Menser, Madisonville, Kentucky

This savory Italian soup relies on items most cooks have in the kitchen, including pasta, prepared spaghetti sauce, canned and frozen vegetables and frozen meatballs. The chunky mixture only needs to simmer for a few minutes.

- 1 cup uncooked spiral *or* shell pasta
- 32 frozen Italian meatballs (about 1 pound), thawed
- 2 cans (14-1/2 ounces *each*) chicken broth
- 1 can (28 ounces) diced tomatoes, undrained
- 1-1/2 cups frozen sliced carrots, thawed
- 1 can (16 ounces) kidney beans, rinsed and drained
- 1 jar (14 ounces) meatless spaghetti sauce
- 1 jar (4-1/2 ounces) sliced mushrooms, drained
- 1 cup frozen peas

Cook pasta according to package directions. Meanwhile, combine the remaining ingredients in a soup kettle or Dutch oven. Bring to a boil; cover and simmer for 5 minutes. Drain pasta and add to the soup; heat through. **Yield:** 10 servings (3 quarts).

Tortellini Vegetable Soup

(Pictured at right)

Deborah Hutchinson, Enfield, Connecticut

Tomatoes, carrots, green beans, potatoes, corn and celery are the perfect complements to convenient frozen tortellini in this heartwarming soup. Add a crusty loaf of bread and a green salad, and dinner is ready in no time.

- 1 large onion chopped
- 2 celery ribs, chopped
- 2 tablespoons vegetable oil
- 2 cans (14-1/2 ounces *each*) beef broth
- 1 cup *each* frozen corn, sliced carrots and cut green beans
- 1 cup diced uncooked potatoes
- 1 teaspoon dried basil
- 1 teaspoon dried thyme
- 1/2 teaspoon minced chives
- 2 cans (14-1/2 ounces *each*) diced tomatoes, undrained
- 2 cups frozen beef *or* cheese tortellini

In a Dutch oven or soup kettle, saute the onion and celery in oil. Add the broth, corn, carrots, beans, potatoes, basil, thyme and chives, and bring to a boil. Reduce heat; cover and simmer for 10-15 minutes or until the potatoes are tender.

Add the tomatoes and tortellini. Simmer, uncovered, for 4-5 minutes or until tortellini is heated through. **Yield:** 10 servings (2-1/2 quarts).

Purchasing Pasta

Whether buying fresh or dried pasta, read the label and only buy brands made with durum wheat (semolina). This is the pasta of preference because it absorbs less water and retains a pleasant "bite" when cooked.

When buying dried pasta, always check the package to make sure the pieces are unbroken. If it looks crumbly or dusty, air has gotten to it, and it's stale.

1 egg
2 tablespoons milk

In a large kettle, combine the first 12 ingredients; bring to a boil. Reduce heat; cover and simmer for 2-1/2 hours or until the chicken is tender. Remove chicken from broth; cool. Debone chicken; cut into chunks. Strain the broth and skim fat; return to the kettle. Add the chicken and carrots.

For noodles, mix flour and salt in a medium bowl. Make a well in the center. Beat egg and milk; pour into the well. Stir together, forming a dough. Turn dough onto a floured surface; knead 8-10 times. Roll into a 12-in. x 9-in. rectangle. Cut into 1/2-in. strips; cut the strips into 1-in. pieces.

Bring soup to a simmer; add noodles. Cover and cook for 12-15 minutes or until noodles are tender. **Yield:** 10-12 servings.

Hearty Chicken Noodle Soup

(Pictured above)

Cindy Renfrow, Sussex, New Jersey

I'm grateful that my mother taught me to make these wonderful old-fashioned noodles, which were a big favorite of mine when I was growing up. They give the chicken soup a delightful down-home flavor.

1 stewing chicken (about 6 pounds), cut up
2 quarts water
1 large onion, quartered
1 cup chopped fresh parsley
1 celery rib, sliced
5 chicken bouillon cubes
5 whole peppercorns
4 whole cloves
1 bay leaf
2 teaspoons salt
1/2 teaspoon pepper
Dash dried thyme
2 medium carrots, thinly sliced
NOODLES:
1-1/4 cups all-purpose flour
1/2 teaspoon salt

Peasant Pasta Soup

Eileen Snider, Cincinnati, Ohio

When I was trying to duplicate a favorite restaurant recipe, I came up with this hearty soup. Pork, pasta, vegetables and beans in a thick tomato broth make it a warm and satisfying supper. My husband and I love the savory Italian flavor.

1-1/2 cups beef broth
2 celery ribs, chopped
2 large carrots, cut into 1/4-inch slices
1 medium onion, chopped
1 can (46 ounces) V8 juice
1 can (14-1/2 ounces) Italian diced tomatoes, undrained
2 cans (6 ounces *each*) Italian tomato paste
1 tablespoon dried oregano
1-1/2 teaspoons pepper
1/4 teaspoon garlic powder
3/4 pound ground pork
3/4 cup canned kidney beans, rinsed and drained
3/4 cup canned great northern beans, rinsed and drained

1 cup medium shell pasta, cooked and drained
Shredded Parmesan cheese

In a large saucepan, combine the broth, celery, carrots and onion. Bring to a boil. Reduce heat; cover and simmer for 5-7 minutes or until vegetables are crisp-tender. Stir in the V8 juice, tomatoes, tomato paste, oregano, pepper and garlic powder. Cover and simmer for 40-45 minutes.

Meanwhile, in a skillet, cook pork over medium heat until no longer pink; drain. Add meat and beans to soup; cover and simmer 30-45 minutes longer or until heated through. Stir in pasta just before serving. Garnish with Parmesan cheese. **Yield:** 8 servings.

Broccoli-Cheese Noodle Soup

Trinity Nicholas, Mt. Carbon, West Virginia

My husband's aunt shared the recipe for this creamy soup, which tastes like you spent all day cooking. It's very filling served with a salad and bread alongside. We like to spoon the leftovers over baked potatoes.

1 package (10 ounces) frozen chopped broccoli
2 ounces angel hair pasta, broken into small pieces
1/4 cup butter
1 tablespoon all-purpose flour
1 cup water
3/4 cup milk
1/8 teaspoon pepper
6 ounces process cheese (Velveeta), cubed
1/2 cup sour cream

Cook both the broccoli and pasta according to package directions; drain. In a large saucepan, melt butter; stir in flour until smooth. Gradually stir in the water, milk and pepper until blended. Bring to a boil; cook and stir for 2 minutes or until thickened.

Reduce heat; stir in cheese until melted. Stir in the broccoli, pasta and sour cream; heat through (do not boil). **Yield:** 4-5 servings.

Beefy Tomato Pasta Soup

(Pictured below)

Nancy Rollag, Kewaskum, Wisconsin

If you're a fan of Italian fare, you'll like this chunky combination.

1 pound ground beef
2 medium green peppers, cut into 1-inch chunks
1 medium onion, cut into chunks
2 garlic cloves, minced
5 to 6 cups water
2 cans (14-1/2 ounces *each*) Italian diced tomatoes, undrained
1 can (6 ounces) tomato paste
1 tablespoon brown sugar
2 to 3 teaspoons Italian seasoning
1 teaspoon salt
1/4 teaspoon pepper
2 cups uncooked spiral pasta
Croutons, optional

In a Dutch oven or soup kettle, cook the beef, green peppers, onion and garlic over medium heat until meat is no longer pink; drain. Add the water, tomatoes, tomato paste, brown sugar, Italian seasoning, salt and pepper.

Bring to a boil. Add pasta. Cook for 10-14 minutes or until pasta is tender, stirring occasionally. Serve with croutons if desired. **Yield:** 10 servings (about 2-1/2 quarts).

Turkey Minestrone

(Pictured below and on page 6)

Betty Christensen, Victoria, British Columbia

I love serving this savory soup to lunch guests. Italian turkey sausage gives the broth just the right spice. I never cooked much when I was growing up, so when I got out on my own, I found that great recipes like this can make anyone a good cook.

2/3 cup chopped onion
2 tablespoons vegetable oil
1/2 pound ground turkey
1/2 pound hot Italian turkey sausage links, casings removed
1/2 cup minced fresh parsley
2 garlic cloves, minced
1 teaspoon dried oregano
1 teaspoon dried basil
2 cans (14-1/2 ounces *each*) Italian stewed tomatoes
6 cups chicken broth
1 medium zucchini, sliced
1 package (10 ounces) frozen mixed vegetables
1 can (16 ounces) kidney beans, rinsed and drained

1-1/2 cups cooked elbow macaroni
2 tablespoons cider vinegar
1/2 teaspoon salt
Pinch pepper

In a large kettle over medium heat, saute onion in oil until tender, about 4 minutes. Add the next six ingredients; cook until meat is no longer pink.

Add tomatoes, broth, zucchini and mixed vegetables; cover and cook on low heat for 5 minutes. Add beans, macaroni, vinegar, salt and pepper; simmer for 3-4 minutes or until heated through. **Yield:** 16 servings (4 quarts).

Hearty Pasta Tomato Soup

Lydia Kroese, Minnetonka, Minnesota

I adapted the original recipe for this flavorful soup so I could make it in the slow cooker. It's ideal for staff luncheons at the school where I work, since we don't have easy access to a stove or oven.

1 pound bulk Italian sausage
6 cups beef broth
1 can (28 ounces) stewed tomatoes
1 can (15 ounces) tomato sauce
2 cups sliced zucchini
1 large onion, chopped
1 cup sliced carrots
1 cup sliced fresh mushrooms
1 medium green pepper, chopped
1/4 cup minced fresh parsley
2 teaspoons sugar
1 teaspoon dried oregano
1 teaspoon dried basil
1 garlic clove, minced
2 cups frozen cheese tortellini
Grated Parmesan cheese, optional

In a skillet, cook the sausage over medium heat until no longer pink; drain. Transfer to a 5-qt. slow cooker; add the next 13 ingredients. Cover and cook on high for 3-4 hours or until the vegetables are tender.

Cook tortellini according to package directions; drain. Stir into slow cooker; cover and cook 30 minutes longer. Serve with Parmesan cheese if desired. **Yield:** 14 servings (about 3-1/2 quarts).

Pasta Sausage Soup

Alice Rabe, Beemer, Nebraska

This is a good soup for our area since we have many good sausage makers. The soup has a rich flavor and is even tastier the next day after the flavors have had time to blend.

1-1/2 pounds hot *or* sweet Italian sausage
1 medium onion, chopped
1 medium green pepper, cut into strips
1 garlic clove, minced
1 can (28 ounces) diced tomatoes, undrained
2 to 2-1/2 cups uncooked bow tie pasta
6 cups water
1 tablespoon sugar
1 tablespoon Worcestershire sauce
2 chicken bouillon cubes
1 teaspoon dried basil
1 teaspoon dried thyme
1 teaspoon salt

Remove casings from the sausages and cut into 1-in. pieces. In a Dutch oven, cook sausage over medium heat until no longer pink. Remove sausage and drain all but 2 tablespoons of the drippings. Saute onion, pepper and garlic until tender. Add sausage and all remaining ingredients. Simmer, uncovered, stirring occasionally until pasta is tender, about 15-20 minutes. **Yield:** 3 quarts.

Pasta in Soups

When preparing pasta to be used in a dish requiring further cooking—such as a soup or casserole—reduce the cooking time by a third. The pasta will continue to cook and absorb liquid in the final dish.

Lasagna Soup

(Pictured above)

Gladys Shaffer, Elma, Washington

This recipe is excellent for working mothers because it's fast to make and very flavorful. Fresh zucchini and corn add color and crunch to a boxed lasagna dinner mix.

1 pound ground beef
1/2 cup chopped onion
1 package (7-3/4 ounces) lasagna dinner mix
5 cups water
1 can (14-1/2 ounces) diced tomatoes, undrained
1 can (7 ounces) whole kernel corn, undrained
2 tablespoons grated Parmesan cheese
1 small zucchini, chopped

In a Dutch oven or soup kettle, cook beef and onion over medium heat until meat is no longer pink; drain. Add contents of lasagna dinner sauce mix, water, tomatoes, corn and Parmesan cheese; bring to a boil.

Reduce heat; cover and simmer for 10 minutes, stirring occasionally. Add the lasagna noodles and zucchini. Cover and simmer for 10 minutes or until noodles are tender. Serve immediately. **Yield:** 10 servings (2-1/2 quarts).

Salads

Cashew Turkey Pasta Salad (p. 23)

Sweet-Sour Pasta Salad

(Pictured above)

Launa Shoemaker, Midland City, Alabama

Fresh garden vegetables add color and crunch to this attractive salad. Its pleasant vinaigrette-type dressing is sparked with ground mustard and garlic. I like the look of the tricolor spirals, but you can substitute other pasta shapes.

1 package (16 ounces) tricolor spiral pasta
1 medium red onion, chopped
1 medium tomato, chopped
1 medium cucumber, peeled, seeded and chopped
1 medium green pepper, chopped
2 tablespoons minced fresh parsley

DRESSING:

1-1/2 cups sugar
1/2 cup vinegar
1 tablespoon ground mustard
1 teaspoon salt
1 teaspoon garlic powder

Cook pasta according to package directions; drain and rinse with cold water. Place in a large serving bowl. Add the onion, tomato, cucumber, green pepper and parsley; set aside.

In a saucepan, combine the dressing ingredients. Cook over medium-low heat for 10 minutes or until sugar is dissolved. Pour over salad and toss to coat. Cover and refrigerate for 2 hours. Serve with a slotted spoon. **Yield:** 16 servings.

Hot Tortellini Salad

Catherine Allan, Twin Falls, Idaho

Once you've cooked the tortellini, the rest of this salad is a breeze to finish in the microwave. Sour cream provides the mild coating over this memorable medley of pasta, ham and broccoli.

1 package (9 ounces) refrigerated cheese tortellini
2 cups fresh broccoli florets
4 to 5 green onions, sliced
2 tablespoons butter
6 ounces fully cooked ham, julienned
1/2 cup sour cream
1 teaspoon dried basil

Cook tortellini according to package directions. Meanwhile, in a 2-qt. microwave-safe bowl, combine broccoli, onions and butter. Cover; microwave on high 2-1/2 minutes. Stir; cook 2-1/2 minutes longer or until broccoli is tender.

Storing Pasta

Dried pasta will last almost indefinitely if stored in an airtight container in a cool, dry place. Dried whole wheat pasta is the exception, and may turn rancid if stored for more than 1 month.

Fresh or refrigerated pasta can be stored in an airtight container in the refrigerator for up to 5 days or in the freezer for up to 8 months.

Keep frozen pasta in the freezer for up to 8 months. It should go directly from the freezer to boiling water.

Drain tortellini. Stir tortellini, ham, sour cream and basil into broccoli mixture. Cover and microwave on high for 1-2 minutes or until heated through. Let stand for 2 minutes before serving. **Yield:** 6-8 servings.

Editor's Note: This recipe was tested in an 850-watt microwave.

Spinach Pasta Salad

Ruby Pyles, Myersville, Maryland

Spinach never lasts that long in my home. We grow spinach and harvest it early in June. We use it in lots of dishes because it's so flavorful and tender. This salad is one of our favorites.

4 cups torn fresh spinach
4 cups cooked spiral pasta
4 cups cubed cooked chicken
2-1/2 cups sliced celery
2 cups green grapes, halved
1 cup fresh snow peas
1 medium tomato, chopped
3 green onions, sliced

DRESSING:

1/2 cup vegetable oil
1/4 cup sugar
2 tablespoons vinegar
2 tablespoons minced fresh parsley
1 teaspoon salt
1 teaspoon lemon juice
1/2 teaspoon finely chopped onion

In a large bowl, combine the first eight ingredients. In a small bowl, whisk together dressing ingredients; pour over salad and toss to coat. Serve immediately. **Yield:** 12-16 servings.

Greek Pasta Salad

(Pictured at right)

Dawna Waggoner, Minong, Wisconsin

Chock-full of tomato, red and green pepper and tricolor spirals, this full-flavored salad is as attractive as it is delicious. I add feta cheese and black olives to the medley before coating it with a speedy homemade dressing.

3 cups uncooked tricolor spiral pasta
1 medium tomato, cut into wedges
1 small sweet red pepper, julienned
1 small green pepper, julienned
4 ounces crumbled feta cheese
1/2 cup sliced ripe olives

DRESSING:

2/3 cup olive oil
1/4 cup minced fresh basil
3 tablespoons white vinegar
2 tablespoons chopped green onions
2 tablespoons grated Parmesan cheese
1/2 teaspoon salt
1/4 teaspoon pepper
1/4 teaspoon dried oregano

Cook the pasta according to package directions; rinse in cold water and drain. Place in a large serving bowl; add the tomato, peppers, feta cheese and olives.

In a blender, combine the dressing ingredients; cover and process until smooth. Pour over salad; toss to coat. Cover and refrigerate for 2 hours or overnight. Toss before serving. **Yield:** 10-12 servings.

Summer Spaghetti Salad

(Pictured top right)

Lucia Johnson, Massena, New York

At summertime picnics, barbecues and reunions, pasta salads are popular fare. This attractive, fresh-tasting salad can conveniently be made the night before. The recipe yields a big bowl!

1 package (16 ounces) thin spaghetti, halved
3 medium tomatoes, diced
3 small zucchini, diced
1 large cucumber, halved, seeded and diced
1 medium green pepper, diced
1 medium sweet red pepper, diced
1 bottle (8 ounces) Italian salad dressing
2 tablespoons grated Parmesan cheese
1-1/2 teaspoons sesame seeds
1-1/2 teaspoons poppy seeds
1/2 teaspoon paprika
1/4 teaspoon celery seed
1/8 teaspoon garlic powder

Cook spaghetti according to package directions; drain and rinse in cold water. Place in a large bowl; add tomatoes, zucchini, cucumber and peppers.

Combine remaining ingredients; pour over salad and toss to coat. Cover and refrigerate for at least 2 hours. **Yield:** 16 servings.

Pasta Fruit Salad

(Pictured middle right)

Dixie Terry, Marion, Illinois

When I serve this unusual but delicious salad at a buffet dinner or picnic, it always draws favorable comments. It's a tasty complement to most any main dish and makes a refreshing dessert.

3 cups uncooked medium pasta shells
1 can (20 ounces) unsweetened pineapple chunks, drained
1 large navel orange, peeled, sectioned and halved
1 cup halved red grapes
1 cup halved green grapes
1 medium apple, chopped
1 large firm banana, cut into 1/4-inch slices
1 carton (8 ounces) plain yogurt
1/4 cup orange juice concentrate

Cook pasta according to package directions; drain and rinse in cold water. Place in a large bowl; add the fruit.

Combine the yogurt and orange juice concentrate; pour over the salad and toss to coat. Cover and refrigerate for several hours. **Yield:** 10 servings.

Oriental Pasta Salad

(Pictured bottom right)

Diane Molberg, Emerald Park, Saskatchewan

With a wonderful combination of colors and flavors, this pasta salad goes great with barbecued chicken or pork. We even like it served with a roll on the side as a meal by itself during the warmer months.

2 cups uncooked elbow macaroni
2 large carrots, cut into 1-inch strips
1 cup snow peas, halved
2 green onions with tops, sliced
1/2 cup thinly sliced sweet red pepper

DRESSING:

1/2 cup mayonnaise
1/2 cup sour cream
1 tablespoon red wine vinegar
1 tablespoon soy sauce
1/2 teaspoon ground ginger
1/4 teaspoon pepper

Cook macaroni according to package directions; drain and rinse in cold water. Place in a large bowl; add the carrots, peas, onions and red pepper.

In a small bowl, whisk dressing ingredients until smooth. Pour over salad and toss to coat. Cover and refrigerate for 1-2 hours. **Yield:** 7 servings.

Ham Macaroni Salad

(Pictured above)

Karen Ballance, Wolf Lake, Illinois

I made some changes to the original recipe by adding extra tomatoes for more color, celery for crunch, relish for a hint of sweetness and ham to make it more filling. It's great for picnics and potlucks or as a side dish for any meal.

1 package (7-1/2 ounces) macaroni and cheese
1/2 cup mayonnaise
2 tablespoons Dijon mustard
3 medium tomatoes, seeded and chopped
1 medium cucumber, peeled and chopped
1 cup diced fully cooked ham
4 hard-cooked eggs, chopped
1/2 cup chopped celery
1/4 cup sweet pickle relish
2 tablespoons chopped onion
1/2 teaspoon salt
1/8 teaspoon pepper

Prepare macaroni and cheese according to package directions; cool for 20 minutes. Stir in the mayonnaise and mustard. Fold in the remaining ingredients. Refrigerate for 2 hours or until chilled. **Yield:** 8 servings.

Cool Cucumber Pasta

Jeanette Fuehring, Concordia, Missouri

People say this salad is crispy, sweet and deliciously different.

8 ounces tube pasta
1 tablespoon vegetable oil
2 medium cucumbers, thinly sliced
1 medium onion, thinly sliced
1-1/2 cups sugar
1 cup water
3/4 cup vinegar
1 tablespoon prepared mustard
1 tablespoon dried parsley flakes
1 teaspoon salt
1 teaspoon pepper
1/2 teaspoon garlic salt

Cook the pasta according to package directions; drain and rinse in cold water. Place in a large bowl; stir in oil, cucumbers and onion.

Combine remaining ingredients; pour over salad and toss. Cover and chill for 3-4 hours, stirring occasionally. Serve with a slotted spoon. **Yield:** 8-10 servings.

Pasta in Salads

When making pasta salad, always slightly undercook the pasta. This will allow the pasta to absorb some of the dressing and still be firm, not mushy.

Hot pasta can be combined with vinaigrette dressing, but let it cool to room temperature before adding other ingredients (fresh herbs, vegetables, etc.) to keep them from wilting.

If you're using long noodles in pasta salad, it's a good idea to rinse them under cold running water to remove excess starch. It's the starch that makes the noodles stick together in unwieldy clumps.

Cashew Turkey Pasta Salad

(Pictured on page 16)

Karen Wyffels, Lino Lakes, Minnesota

Cashews add a nice crunch to this grilled turkey and spiral pasta combo. I first tasted this salad at a baby shower and asked the hostess for her recipe. Since then, I've served it for many occasions over the years.

- **2 bone-in turkey breast halves, skin removed**
- **3 cups uncooked tricolor spiral pasta**
- **2 celery ribs, diced**
- **6 green onions, chopped**
- **1/2 cup diced green pepper**
- **1-1/2 cups mayonnaise**
- **3/4 cup packed brown sugar**
- **1 tablespoon cider vinegar**
- **1-1/2 teaspoons salt**
- **1-1/2 teaspoons lemon juice**
- **2 cups salted cashew halves**

Grill turkey, covered, over medium heat for 25-30 minutes on each side or until juices run clear. Cool slightly. Cover and refrigerate until cool. Meanwhile, cook pasta according to package directions; drain and rinse in cold water.

Chop turkey; place in a large bowl. Add the pasta, celery, onions and green pepper. In a small bowl, combine the mayonnaise, brown sugar, vinegar, salt and lemon juice; pour over pasta mixture and toss to coat. Cover and refrigerate for at least 2 hours. Just before serving, stir in cashews. **Yield:** 12 servings.

Salami Pasta Salad

(Pictured at right)

Marion Lowery, Medford, Oregon

Popular any time of the year, this crowd-pleasing pasta salad is especially perfect for summer picnics. Made the day before, it has a pleasant vinaigrette dressing sparked with herbs. I set aside the Parmesan cheese and add it just before the salad is served.

- **3 cups uncooked medium tube pasta *or* elbow macaroni**
- **1/2 pound bulk hard salami *or* summer sausage, cubed**
- **1/2 cup minced fresh parsley**
- **4 green onions, sliced**
- **1/2 cup olive oil**
- **1/4 cup red wine vinegar**
- **4 teaspoons minced fresh oregano *or* 1 teaspoon dried oregano**
- **4 teaspoons minced fresh basil *or* 1 teaspoon dried basil**
- **2 garlic cloves, minced**
- **1 teaspoon salt**
- **1/4 teaspoon pepper**
- **1/2 cup shredded Parmesan cheese**

In a saucepan, cook pasta according to package directions; rinse in cold water and drain. Place in a large bowl; add salami, parsley and onions.

In a small bowl, whisk together oil, vinegar and seasonings. Drizzle over pasta mixture and toss to coat. Cover and refrigerate overnight. Just before serving, stir in Parmesan cheese. **Yield:** 8 servings.

Picnic Pasta Salad

(Pictured below)

Felicia Fiocchi, Vineland, New Jersey

My family's not big on traditional pasta salads made with mayonnaise, so when I served this colorful version that uses Italian dressing, it was a big hit. This crowd-pleaser is loaded with vegetables, beans and tricolor pasta.

1 package (12 ounces) tricolor spiral pasta
1 package (10 ounces) refrigerated tricolor tortellini
1 jar (7 ounces) marinated artichoke hearts, undrained
1/2 pound fresh broccoli florets (about 1-3/4 cups)
12 ounces provolone cheese, cubed
12 ounces hard salami, cubed
1 medium sweet red pepper, chopped
1 medium green pepper, chopped
1 can (15 ounces) garbanzo beans *or* chickpeas, rinsed and drained
2 cans (2-1/4 ounces *each*) sliced ripe olives, drained
1 medium red onion, chopped
4 garlic cloves, minced
2 envelopes Italian salad dressing mix

Cook spiral pasta and tortellini according to package directions. Drain and rinse in cold water. Place in a large bowl; add the artichokes, broccoli, provolone cheese, salami, peppers, beans, olives, onion and garlic.

Prepare salad dressing according to package directions; pour over salad and toss to coat. Serve immediately or refrigerate. **Yield:** 14-16 servings.

Sour Cream Macaroni Salad

Rita Morris, Gastonia, North Carolina

This make-ahead macaroni salad never fails to stay moist. I double the recipe for large groups.

1 package (8 ounces) elbow macaroni
3/4 cup diced green pepper
1/3 cup sweet pickle relish
1 jar (2 ounces) diced pimientos, drained
1 tablespoon grated onion
1/2 cup mayonnaise
1/2 cup sour cream
1/4 cup milk
1-1/2 teaspoons salt
Pepper to taste

Cook macaroni according to package directions; rinse in cold water and drain. Place in a large bowl; add green pepper, pickle relish, pimientos and onion.

In a small bowl, combine the remaining ingredients; mix well. Pour over macaroni mixture and toss to coat. Cover and refrigerate until serving. **Yield:** 6 servings.

Italian Pasta Salad

Tina Dierking, Canaan, Maine

This zesty recipe combines vegetables and pasta in a creamy dressing. Refreshing and filling, this change-of-pace salad is perfect as a side dish. It's always popular at a potluck.

- **3/4 cup uncooked spiral pasta**
- **1-1/2 cups halved cherry tomatoes**
- **1 cup sliced fresh mushrooms**
- **1/4 cup chopped sweet red pepper**
- **1/4 cup chopped green pepper**
- **3 tablespoons thinly sliced green onions**
- **1-1/2 cups zesty Italian salad dressing**
- **3/4 cup mayonnaise**
- **1/2 cup grated Parmesan cheese**
- **1/3 cup cubed provolone cheese**
- **1 can (2-1/4 ounces) sliced ripe olives, drained**
- **Leaf lettuce, optional**

Cook pasta according to package directions; rinse with cold water and drain. Place in a bowl; add the tomatoes, mushrooms, peppers, onions and salad dressing. Cover and refrigerate for at least 4 hours or overnight; drain.

In a bowl, combine mayonnaise and Parmesan cheese; stir in provolone cheese and olives. Gently fold into pasta mixture. Serve in a lettuce-lined bowl if desired. **Yield:** 6 servings.

Kielbasa Pasta Salad

(Pictured above right)

Jean Dantinne, Chehalis, Washington

The sausage adds wonderful flavor and heartiness to this main-dish salad. But the real secret to its appeal is the crunchy croutons.

- **1 package (16 ounces) spiral pasta**
- **1-1/2 cups thinly sliced fully cooked kielbasa *or* Polish sausage**
- **1 can (2-1/4 ounces) sliced ripe olives, drained**
- **1/4 cup shredded Parmesan cheese**
- **1 cup mayonnaise**
- **3 tablespoons cider vinegar**
- **1 envelope Italian salad dressing mix**
- **1 cup salad croutons**

Cook pasta according to package directions; drain and rinse in cold water. Place pasta in a large bowl; add the sausage, olives and Parmesan cheese.

In a small bowl, combine the mayonnaise, vinegar and salad dressing mix. Stir into the pasta mixture. Add croutons and toss to coat. Serve immediately. **Yield:** 12 servings.

Pasta Math

How much pasta to buy per serving depends on whether it's fresh or dried (fresh pasta is heavier because it contains moisture).

For dried pasta, allow 2 ounces per side-dish serving and 4 ounces per main-dish serving. But for fresh pasta, allow 3 ounces per side-dish serving and 5 ounces per main-dish serving.

One pound of dried macaroni-style pasta (shells, elbows, etc.) equals about 9 cups cooked. One pound of dried spaghetti-style noodles equals about 7 cups cooked.

Spicy Ravioli Salad

(Pictured above)

Paula Marchesi, Lenhartsville, Pennsylvania

This is a convenient combination of frozen ravioli and pantry staples is dressed with taco sauce for tangy, fresh-tasting results.

1 package (25 ounces) frozen beef, sausage *or* cheese ravioli
1 can (10 ounces) diced tomatoes and green chilies, undrained
1 can (8-3/4 ounces) whole kernel corn, drained
1 bottle (8 ounces) taco sauce
1 can (2-1/4 ounces) sliced ripe olives, drained
1 small cucumber, peeled, seeded and chopped
1 small red onion, sliced
2 garlic cloves, minced
1/4 teaspoon ground cumin
1/4 teaspoon salt
1/4 teaspoon pepper

Cook ravioli according to package directions. Meanwhile, combine remaining ingredients in a large bowl. Drain ravioli; stir into tomato mixture. Cover and refrigerate for at least 2 hours. **Yield:** 8-10 servings.

Angel Hair Pasta Salad

Kimberly Garner, Batesville, Arkansas

A light vinegar-and-oil dressing allows the fresh flavors of tomatoes, carrots and cucumber to shine through in this easy-to-assemble salad. Toss in cubed cooked chicken for a complete meal.

1 package (7 ounces) angel hair pasta
4 plum tomatoes, seeded and chopped
1 cup thinly sliced carrots
1 medium cucumber, chopped
6 green onions, thinly sliced
2 tablespoons olive *or* canola oil
2 tablespoons cider vinegar
1/2 teaspoon salt
1/4 teaspoon pepper

Cook pasta according to package directions; drain and rinse in cold water. Place in a large bowl; add the tomatoes, carrots, cucumber and onions. In a small bowl, whisk together the oil, vinegar, salt and pepper. Pour over pasta mixture and toss to coat. Cover and refrigerate for 4 hours. **Yield:** 8 servings.

Colorful Linguine Salad

Lee Ann Berijan, Blaine, Minnesota

For a long time, my family has been trying to cut down on high-fat foods. I've tried to use my creativity and my family's love of pasta to provide tasty meals. This satisfying dish is great after a day in the summer sun.

1 medium zucchini, thinly sliced
1/2 cup julienned carrots
1/2 cup fresh *or* frozen pea pods
3 cups cooked linguine
3/4 cup julienned sweet red pepper

DRESSING:

3 tablespoons white wine vinegar *or* cider vinegar
2 tablespoons olive *or* canola oil
2 teaspoons Dijon mustard

1 garlic clove, minced
1 teaspoon sugar
1 teaspoon dried thyme, optional
1/2 teaspoon salt
1/4 teaspoon white pepper

Place the zucchini and carrots in a steamer basket; place in a saucepan over 1 in. of water. Bring to a boil; cover and steam for 2-3 minutes. Add the pea pods; steam for 1 minute. Transfer the vegetables to a large bowl; add the linguine and red pepper.

In a small bowl, whisk together the dressing ingredients. Pour over linguine mixture and toss to coat. Cover and refrigerate for 1 hour or until serving. **Yield:** 4 servings.

Sausage Bow Tie Salad

Christina Campeau, Simi Valley, California

I made this flavorful entree salad for a first date. My boyfriend liked it so much, he took the leftovers home—and his roommates raved about it. For a change of pace, you can substitute turkey sausage for the kielbasa.

1 pound fully cooked reduced-fat kielbasa *or* Polish sausage, cut into 1/4-inch slices
1 large onion, finely chopped
1 tablespoon water
1-1/2 teaspoons minced garlic, *divided*
1/2 cup balsamic vinegar
1 to 3 teaspoons fennel seed, crushed
5 cups cooked bow tie pasta
7 plum tomatoes, diced
1/4 cup minced fresh basil *or* 4 teaspoons dried basil
1 cup (4 ounces) crumbled feta cheese

In a large nonstick skillet, cook the sausage, onion, water and 3/4 teaspoon garlic over medium heat for 10 minutes. Add the vinegar and fennel seed. Reduce heat; cover and simmer for 5 minutes. Remove from the heat. Stir in pasta until coated. Add the tomatoes, basil and remaining garlic; stir gently. Cover and refrigerate until serving. Sprinkle with feta cheese. **Yield:** 9 servings.

Crab-Salad Jumbo Shells

(Pictured below)

JoAnne Anderson, Knoxville, Iowa

I received this recipe from a friend and adjusted the ingredients to suit my family's tastes. It's a fun and flavorful way to serve crab salad.

30 jumbo pasta shells
1 cup finely chopped fresh broccoli florets
1 garlic clove, minced
2 packages (8 ounces *each*) imitation crabmeat, chopped
1 cup (8 ounces) sour cream
1/2 cup mayonnaise
1/4 cup finely shredded carrot
1/4 cup diced seeded peeled cucumber
1 tablespoon chopped green onion
1 teaspoon dill weed

Cook pasta according to package directions; rinse in cold water and drain well. In a microwave-safe bowl, combine the broccoli and garlic. Cover and microwave on high for 1 minute or until crisp-tender. Transfer to a large bowl; stir in the remaining ingredients. Stuff into pasta shells. Cover and refrigerate overnight. **Yield:** 30 stuffed shells.

Side Di

Never-Fail Egg Noodles (p. 32)

Mushroom Pasta Pilaf

(Pictured above)

Jennifer McQuillan, Jacksonville, Florida

This simmered side dish is an excellent complement to shish kabobs or any beef main dish. Tiny pieces of pasta pick up bold seasoning from mushrooms, onions and Worcestershire sauce. It makes a delightful change of pace from more traditional side dishes.

1 small onion, chopped
1/4 cup butter
1-1/3 cups uncooked ring, orzo *or* other small pasta
1 can (10-1/2 ounces) beef consomme, undiluted
1 cup water
1 can (7 ounces) mushroom stems and pieces, undrained
1 tablespoon Worcestershire sauce
1 teaspoon salt
1/4 teaspoon soy sauce
Dash pepper

In a large skillet, saute onion in butter until tender. Add remaining ingredients; bring to a boil. Reduce heat; cover and simmer for 20 minutes or until the pasta is tender and liquid is absorbed. **Yield:** 6-8 servings.

Summer Garden Pasta

April Johnson, Tonasket, Washington

This fresh-tasting side dish pairs pasta with an array of nutritious veggies, including zucchini, bell peppers and a juicy tomato. Our four boys are all grown and out of the house, but I still grow a large garden every summer and give away everything we can't eat.

1 package (1 pound) small shell pasta
1 cup sliced yellow summer squash
1 cup sliced zucchini
1 cup julienned sweet red pepper
1 cup julienned green pepper
1 cup sliced green onions
6 garlic cloves, peeled and thinly sliced
1/4 cup butter
1-1/2 cups chicken broth
1 small tomato, chopped
1/2 cup grated Parmesan cheese
1 tablespoon minced fresh parsley
2 teaspoons garlic pepper
1 teaspoon salt

Cook pasta according to package directions. Meanwhile, in a large skillet, saute the yellow squash, zucchini, peppers, onions and garlic in

Pasta Substitutes

Pasta with similar sizes and shapes (like spaghetti and vermicelli or elbow macaroni and small shells) are interchangeable in most recipes.

Cook only one type of pasta at a time. If you prepare two varieties together, one is likely to be done before the other. Fresh pastas (like tortellini and ravioli) cook faster than their dried counterparts.

butter until crisp-tender. Add broth and tomato; bring to a boil. Cook and stir until liquid is reduced by half.

Drain pasta; stir into vegetable mixture. Cook 1 minute longer or until heated through. Transfer to a large bowl. Sprinkle with Parmesan cheese, parsley, garlic pepper and salt; toss to coat. Serve immediately. **Yield:** 9 servings.

Lemon Broccoli Pasta

Margaret Fuhrman, Erie, Pennsylvania

This pleasant pasta toss is delicious, simple to make and uses just one saucepan. My family and friends really like it, so I serve it often.

- **2 cans (14-1/2 ounces *each*) chicken broth**
- **1 teaspoon lemon juice**
- **1 teaspoon grated lemon peel**
- **1/4 teaspoon garlic powder**
- **1/4 teaspoon pepper**
- **6 ounces uncooked angel hair pasta**
- **3 cups broccoli florets**
- **3/4 cup sour cream**
- **2 tablespoons grated Parmesan cheese**

In a saucepan, combine the broth, lemon juice and peel, garlic powder and pepper. Bring to a boil. Add pasta and broccoli.

Reduce heat; simmer, uncovered, for 3-4 minutes or until the pasta is tender. Drain; stir in the sour cream. Sprinkle with the cheese. **Yield:** 4 servings.

Cheesy Noodle Casserole

(Pictured at right)

Shirley McKee, Varna, Illinois

This rich, cheesy side dish is such a great meal extender that I always keep it in mind whenever I feel my menu needs a boost. It's a quick and easy casserole to fix...and is always devoured in a hurry!

- **2 packages (1 pound *each*) wide egg noodles**
- **1/2 cup butter**
- **1/4 cup all-purpose flour**
- **1 teaspoon garlic salt**
- **1 teaspoon onion salt**
- **5 to 6 cups milk**
- **2 pounds process cheese (Velveeta), cubed**

TOPPING:

- **1/2 cup dry bread crumbs**
- **2 tablespoons butter, melted**

Cook noodles according to package directions; drain. In a Dutch oven, melt butter. Stir in the flour, garlic salt and onion salt until smooth. Gradually stir in milk. Bring to a boil; cook and stir for 2 minutes or until thickened and bubbly. Add the cheese; stir until melted. Stir in the noodles.

Transfer to two greased shallow 2-qt. baking dishes. Toss bread crumbs and butter; sprinkle over casseroles. Bake, uncovered, at 350° for 25-30 minutes or until golden brown. **Yield:** 2 casseroles (12 servings each).

Tomato Spiral Toss

(Pictured below)

Nicole Lynch, Powell River, British Columbia

When my husband and I don't have a lot of time, we fix this pleasing pasta side dish that's easy to prepare.

8 ounces uncooked spiral pasta
2-1/2 cups diced fresh tomatoes
1 tablespoon dried basil
1/4 to 1/2 cup vegetable oil
2 tablespoons cider vinegar
2 garlic cloves, minced
1/4 teaspoon salt
1/8 teaspoon pepper
3 tablespoons grated Parmesan cheese

Cook pasta according to package directions. Meanwhile, combine tomatoes and basil in a serving bowl; set aside. In a small bowl, combine the oil, vinegar, garlic, salt and pepper.

Drain pasta; add to tomato mixture. Drizzle with oil mixture and toss to coat. Sprinkle with Parmesan cheese. Serve immediately. **Yield:** 6 servings.

Never-Fail Egg Noodles

(Pictured on page 28)

Kathryn Roach, Greers Ferry, Arkansas

Some 30 years ago, the small church I attended held a chicken and noodle fund-raiser supper. I was put in charge of noodles for 200 people! A dear lady shared this recipe and said it had been tried and tested by countless cooks. These noodles are just plain good eating!

1 egg plus 3 egg yolks
3 tablespoons cold water
1 teaspoon salt
2 cups all-purpose flour
Chopped fresh parsley, optional

In a mixing bowl, beat egg and yolks until light and fluffy. Add water and salt; mix well. Stir in flour. Turn onto a floured surface; knead until smooth. Divide into thirds. Roll out each portion to 1/8-in. thickness. Cut noodles to desired width.

Cook immediately in boiling salted water or chicken broth for 7-9 minutes or until tender. Drain; sprinkle with parsley if desired. **Yield:** about 5-1/2 cups.

Editor's Note: Uncooked noodles may be stored in the refrigerator for 2-3 days or frozen for up to 1 month.

Garlic Parsley Spaghetti

Evelyn Sparish, Cumberland, Wisconsin

This simple recipe calls for only a few ingredients. I combine pasta, garlic and parsley to create the versatile savory dish.

1 package (16 ounces) thin spaghetti
4 garlic cloves, minced
1/2 cup olive oil
1/2 cup minced fresh parsley
Salt and pepper to taste

Cook spaghetti according to package directions. Meanwhile, in a large skillet, lightly brown garlic in oil over medium heat. Drain spaghetti; add to the skillet. Sprinkle with parsley, salt and pepper; toss to coat. **Yield:** 8-10 servings.

Broccoli Noodle Side Dish

Louise Saluti, Sandwich, Massachusetts

This pasta side dish is both colorful and satisfying. Plus, it goes well with a variety of main dishes.

6 cups (8 ounces) uncooked wide noodles
3 to 4 garlic cloves, minced
1/4 cup olive oil
4 cups broccoli florets (about 1 pound)
1/2 pound fresh mushrooms, thinly sliced
1/2 teaspoon dried thyme
1/4 teaspoon pepper
1 teaspoon salt

Cook noodles according to package directions. Meanwhile, in a skillet, saute garlic in oil until tender. Add broccoli; saute for 4 minutes or until crisp-tender. Add mushrooms, thyme, pepper and salt; saute for 2-3 minutes. Drain noodles; add to broccoli mixture. Stir gently over low heat until heated through. **Yield:** 8 servings.

Con Queso Spirals

JoAnne Palmer, Mechanicsville, Maryland

This few-ingredient dish is a sure favorite no matter what the main course may be. Spicy Mexican cheese dip from the snack aisle creates a zippy coating for spiral pasta.

2-1/2 cups uncooked spiral pasta
1 tablespoon butter
1 cup salsa con queso dip
Sour cream

Cook pasta according to package directions; drain. Place in a bowl; stir in butter until melted. Stir in con queso dip. Serve with sour cream. **Yield:** 4 servings.

Pepperoni Angel Hair

(Pictured above)

Julie Mosher, Coldwater, Michigan

This noodle side dish is so versatile that it can accompany steak, pork chops, chicken or even hamburgers. Chill leftovers to serve as a cool main-dish salad on a warm summer night. When time allows, I like to replace the pepperoni with sliced cooked chicken.

8 ounces uncooked angel hair pasta, broken into thirds
1 small cucumber, peeled and chopped
1 medium green pepper, chopped
1 package (8 ounces) sliced pepperoni, quartered
2 cans (2-1/4 ounces *each*) sliced ripe olives, drained
1/2 cup Italian salad dressing
1-1/4 cups shredded Parmesan cheese

Cook the pasta according to package directions. Meanwhile, combine the cucumber, green pepper, pepperoni and olives in a large bowl. Drain pasta and add to pepperoni mixture. Top with salad dressing and Parmesan cheese; toss to coat. **Yield:** 4-6 servings.

Tomato Basil Linguine

(Pictured above)

DiAnn Mallehan, Grand Rapids, Michigan

Hot pasta is tossed with a fresh-tasting sauce that includes tomatoes, basil and Brie cheese in this deliciously different side dish. It's very pretty, too. Even when it cools off, this pasta tastes great.

- **1 pound Brie *or* Camembert cheese, rind removed and cut into small pieces**
- **4 large tomatoes, coarsely chopped**
- **1 cup chopped fresh basil**
- **1/2 cup olive oil**
- **3 garlic cloves, minced**
- **1/2 teaspoon salt**
- **1/4 teaspoon white pepper**
- **1-1/2 pounds uncooked linguine**
- **Shredded Parmesan cheese**

In a large serving bowl, combine the first seven ingredients. Let stand at room temperature for up to 1-1/2 hours.

Cook linguine according to package directions; drain. Toss with cheese mixture. Sprinkle with Parmesan cheese. Serve immediately. **Yield:** 10 servings.

Creamy Sprouts 'n' Noodles

Dixie Terry, Marion, Illinois

This comforting casserole is great with pork roast or pork chops. It makes a tasty side dish for company.

- **1 pound fresh brussels sprouts, quartered**
- **2 medium onions, finely chopped**
- **4 tablespoons butter, *divided***
- **1 cup (8 ounces) sour cream**
- **1 cup (8 ounces) small-curd cottage cheese**
- **1 garlic clove, minced**
- **1 teaspoon paprika**
- **1/2 teaspoon salt**
- **1/4 to 1/2 teaspoon caraway seeds**
- **3 cups medium egg noodles, cooked and drained**
- **1 cup soft bread crumbs**

Place the brussels sprouts and a small amount of water in a saucepan; cover and cook until tender. Meanwhile, in a skillet, saute onions in 2 tablespoons butter until golden brown. Remove from the heat; stir in the sour cream, cottage cheese, garlic, paprika, salt and caraway.

Drain sprouts; add to onion mixture with noodles. Spread into a greased shallow 2-qt. baking dish. Melt remaining butter and toss with bread crumbs. Sprinkle over casserole. Bake, uncovered, at 375° for 20-25 minutes or until golden brown. **Yield:** 6-8 servings.

Leftover Pasta

Leftover plain pasta can be refrigerated for 1 to 2 days in an airtight container. Reheat by placing in a colander and rinsing with hot water.

Or make an au gratin side dish by placing leftover plain pasta in a greased shallow baking dish and layering with sauteed mushrooms or green peppers or other vegetables. Moisten with the sauce of your choice and top with bread crumbs and shredded cheese. Bake at 350° for 25 minutes or until warmed through and the top is golden brown.

Artichoke Spinach Shells

Rachel Balsamo, Lewiston, Maine

I found this side dish in a magazine years ago. If you're looking for a vegetarian meal, it's wonderful as the main course served with hot dinner rolls and a salad.

4 cups uncooked medium pasta shells
10 ounces fresh spinach, chopped
3 cups (12 ounces) shredded cheddar cheese
1 can (14-1/2 ounces) Italian stewed tomatoes
1 can (14 ounces) water-packed artichoke hearts, drained and quartered
1 cup (8 ounces) sour cream
1/2 teaspoon garlic salt

In a Dutch oven, cook pasta in boiling water for 5 minutes. Add spinach; cook, uncovered, for 6-8 minutes or until pasta is tender. Drain.

In a large bowl, combine the remaining ingredients. Stir in pasta mixture until blended. Transfer to a 3-qt. baking dish. Bake, uncovered, at 350° for 30-35 minutes or until heated through. **Yield:** 6-8 servings.

Company Mac and Cheese

(Pictured at right)

Catherine Odgen, Middlegrove, New York

This is by far the creamiest, tastiest and most special macaroni and cheese I have ever tried. I'm not usually a fan of homemade macaroni and cheese, but when a friend served this, I had to have the recipe.

1 package (7 ounces) elbow macaroni
6 tablespoons butter, *divided*
3 tablespoons all-purpose flour
2 cups milk
1 package (8 ounces) cream cheese, cubed
2 cups (8 ounces) shredded cheddar cheese
2 teaspoons spicy brown mustard
1/2 teaspoon salt
1/4 teaspoon pepper
3/4 cup dry bread crumbs
2 tablespoons minced fresh parsley

Cook macaroni according to package directions. Meanwhile, melt 4 tablespoons butter in a large saucepan. Stir in flour until smooth. Gradually add milk. Bring to a boil; cook and stir for 2 minutes. Reduce heat; add cheeses, mustard, salt and pepper. Stir until cheese is melted and sauce is smooth.

Drain macaroni; add to the cheese sauce and stir to coat. Transfer to a greased shallow 3-qt. baking dish. Melt the remaining butter; toss with bread crumbs and parsley. Sprinkle over macaroni.

Bake, uncovered, at 400° for 15-20 minutes or until golden brown. **Yield:** 6-8 servings.

Stuffed S
& Manic

Manicotti for Two (p. 45)

Three-Cheese Shells

(Pictured above)

June Barrus, Springville, Utah

These stuffed shells make a hearty meatless entree. The vegetables and three types of cheese bring together contrasting textures and delightful flavors. It's easy to prepare ahead, then bake just in time for dinner.

1 package (12 ounces) jumbo pasta shells
3 cups (24 ounces) ricotta cheese
3 cups (12 ounces) shredded mozzarella cheese
1/2 cup grated Parmesan cheese
1/2 cup chopped green pepper
1/2 cup chopped fresh mushrooms
2 tablespoons dried basil
2 eggs, lightly beaten
2 garlic cloves, minced
1/2 teaspoon seasoned salt
1/4 teaspoon pepper
2 jars (one 28 ounces, one 14 ounces) spaghetti sauce, *divided*

Cook pasta shells according to package directions. Drain and rinse in cold water. In a bowl, combine the next 10 ingredients. Divide the small jar of spaghetti sauce between two ungreased 13-in. x 9-in. x 2-in. baking dishes.

Fill shells with the cheese mixture and place in a single layer over sauce. Pour the remaining spaghetti sauce over the shells. Cover and bake at 350° for 20 minutes. Uncover and bake 10 minutes longer or until heated through. **Yield:** 9 servings.

Homemade Manicotti

Sue Ann Bunt, Painted Post, New York

These tender manicotti are much easier to stuff than the purchased variety. People are always amazed when I say I make my own noodles. My son fixed this recipe for several of his friends, and they were extremely impressed with his cooking skills.

CREPE NOODLES:
1-1/2 cups all-purpose flour
1 cup milk
3 eggs
1/2 teaspoon salt
FILLING:
1-1/2 pounds ricotta cheese
1/4 cup grated Romano cheese
1 egg
1 tablespoon minced fresh parsley *or* 1 teaspoon dried parsley flakes
1 jar (28 ounces) spaghetti sauce
Shredded Romano cheese, optional

Place flour in a bowl; whisk in milk, eggs and salt until smooth. Pour about 2 tablespoons onto a hot greased 8-in. skillet; spread to a 5-in. circle. Cook over medium heat until set; do not brown or turn.

Repeat with remaining batter, making 18 crepes. Stack crepes between waxed paper; set aside.

For filling, combine cheeses, egg and parsley. Spoon 3-4 tablespoons down the center of each crepe; roll up. Pour half of the spaghetti sauce into an ungreased 13-in. x 9-in. x 2-in. baking dish. Place crepes, seam side down, over sauce; pour remaining sauce over top.

Cover and bake at 350° for 20 minutes. Uncover and bake 20 minutes longer or until heated through. Sprinkle with Romano cheese if desired. **Yield:** 6 servings.

Pasta Shells

Instead of draining jumbo pasta shells in a colander, which can cause them to tear, carefully remove them from boiling water with a tongs. Pour out any water inside the shells and drain on lightly greased waxed paper until you're ready to stuff them.

To easily stuff pasta or manicotti shells, place the filling in a large resealable plastic bag; seal the bag. Cut off a small part of one bottom corner. Squeeze the filling into each shell.

Italian Stuffed Shells

Beverly Austin, Fulton, Missouri

A dear friend first brought over this casserole when I was recovering from an accident. Now I take it to other friends' homes and to potlucks.

- **1 pound ground beef**
- **1 cup chopped onion**
- **1 garlic clove, minced**
- **2 cups hot water**
- **1 can (12 ounces) tomato paste**
- **1 tablespoon beef bouillon granules**
- **1-1/2 teaspoons dried oregano**
- **1 carton (16 ounces) cottage cheese**
- **2 cups (8 ounces) shredded mozzarella cheese, *divided***
- **1/2 cup grated Parmesan cheese**
- **1 egg, beaten**
- **24 jumbo shell noodles, cooked and drained**

In a large skillet, cook beef, onion and garlic until meat is no longer pink; drain well. Stir in water, tomato paste, bouillon and oregano; simmer, uncovered, about 30 minutes.

Meanwhile, in a medium bowl, combine cottage cheese, 1 cup mozzarella, Parmesan cheese and egg; mix well. Stuff shells with cheese mixture; arrange in a 13-in. x 9-in. x 2-in. baking dish. Pour meat sauce over shells.

Cover and bake at 350° for 30 minutes. Uncover, sprinkle with remaining mozzarella cheese. Bake 5 minutes longer or until the cheese is melted. **Yield:** 6-8 servings.

Easy-to-Stuff Manicotti

(Pictured below)

Suzanne Runtz, Charleston, South Carolina

Even kids can help assemble this simplified Italian entree. I fill each pasta shell with a piece of string cheese for a deliciously gooey center, then top the manicotti with a beefy tomato sauce.

- **1 package (8 ounces) manicotti shells**
- **1 pound ground beef**
- **1/2 cup chopped onion**
- **1 jar (26 ounces) spaghetti sauce**
- **14 pieces string cheese**
- **1-1/2 cups (6 ounces) shredded mozzarella cheese**

Cook manicotti according to package directions. Meanwhile, in a large skillet, cook beef and onion over medium heat until meat is no longer pink; drain. Stir in the spaghetti sauce. Spread half of the meat sauce into a greased 13-in. x 9-in. x 2-in. baking dish.

Drain manicotti; stuff each shell with a piece of string cheese. Place over meat sauce; top with remaining sauce. Cover and bake at 350° for 25-30 minutes or until heated through. Sprinkle with mozzarella cheese. Bake, uncovered, for 5-10 minutes or until the cheese is melted. **Yield:** 6-8 servings.

Chicken Broccoli Shells

(Pictured below)

Karen Jagger, Columbia City, Indiana

This cheesy entree can be assembled ahead of time and popped in the oven when company arrives. I suggest rounding out the meal with a tossed salad and warm bread. It's a deliciously different way to stuff pasta shells.

- **1 jar (16 ounces) Alfredo sauce**
- **2 cups frozen chopped broccoli, thawed**
- **2 cups diced cooked chicken**
- **1 cup (4 ounces) shredded cheddar cheese**
- **1/4 cup shredded Parmesan cheese**
- **21 jumbo pasta shells, cooked and drained**

In a large bowl, combine the Alfredo sauce, broccoli, chicken and cheeses. Spoon into pasta shells.

Place in a greased 13-in. x 9-in. x 2-in. baking dish. Cover and bake at 350° for 30-35 minutes or until heated through. **Yield:** 7 servings.

Ham-Stuffed Manicotti

Dorothy Anderson, Ottawa, Kansas

Here's a fun and different use for ham. It's unexpected combined with the manicotti, yet tastes delicious. The creamy cheese sauce makes this casserole perfect for chilly days or any time of the year. I'm always asked for the recipe whenever I serve it.

- **8 manicotti shells**
- **1/2 cup chopped onion**
- **1 tablespoon vegetable oil**
- **3 cups (1 pound) ground fully cooked ham**
- **1 can (4 ounces) sliced mushrooms, drained**
- **1 cup (4 ounces) shredded Swiss cheese, *divided***
- **3 tablespoons grated Parmesan cheese**
- **1/4 to 1/2 cup chopped green pepper**
- **3 tablespoons butter**
- **3 tablespoons all-purpose flour**
- **2 cups milk**

Paprika
Chopped fresh parsley

Cook manicotti according to package directions; set aside. In a large skillet, saute onion in oil until tender. Remove from the heat. Add ham, mushrooms, half of the Swiss cheese and Parmesan; set aside.

In a saucepan, saute green pepper in butter until tender. Stir in flour until thoroughly combined. Add milk; cook, stirring constantly, until thickened and bubbly. Mix a quarter of the sauce into ham mixture. Stuff shells with about 1/3 cup of filling each. Place in a greased 11-in. x 7-in. x 2-in. baking dish. Top with remaining sauce; sprinkle with paprika.

Cover and bake at 350° for 30 minutes or until heated through. Sprinkle with parsley and remaining Swiss cheese before serving. **Yield:** 8 servings.

Editor's Note: Recipe can easily be doubled for a larger group.

Alfredo Shrimp Shells

Taste of Home Test Kitchen

Prepared Alfredo sauce streamlines the preparation of these tasty stuffed shells filled with shrimp, mushrooms and green onion.

1/2 cup chopped fresh mushrooms
1 teaspoon butter
1 green onion, sliced
1 package (5 ounces) frozen cooked salad shrimp, thawed
2 tablespoons plus 1/2 cup Alfredo sauce, *divided*
6 jumbo pasta shells, cooked and drained
Lemon wedges and fresh parsley

In a skillet, saute mushrooms in butter until almost tender. Add onion; cook until tender. Stir in the shrimp and 2 tablespoons Alfredo sauce. Pour 1/4 cup of the remaining sauce into a greased 8-in. square baking dish.

Fill each pasta shell with 2 tablespoons shrimp mixture; place in baking dish. Top with the remaining Alfredo sauce. Cover and bake at 350° for 20-25 minutes or until bubbly. Serve with lemon and parsley. **Yield:** 2 servings.

Meaty Spinach Manicotti

(Pictured above right)

Pat Schroeder, Elkhorn, Wisconsin

This hearty stuffed pasta dish will feed a crowd. Tangy tomato sauce tops manicotti that's filled with a mouth-watering blend of Italian sausage, chicken, spinach and mozzarella cheese. Be prepared to share the recipe!

2 packages (8 ounces *each*) manicotti shells
1/4 cup butter
1/4 cup all-purpose flour
2-1/2 cups milk
3/4 cup grated Parmesan cheese
1 pound bulk Italian sausage
4 cups diced cooked chicken *or* turkey
2 packages (10 ounces *each*) frozen chopped spinach, thawed and squeezed dry
2 eggs, beaten
1 cup (4 ounces) shredded mozzarella cheese
2 cans (26-1/2 ounces *each*) spaghetti sauce
1/4 cup minced fresh parsley

Cook manicotti according to package directions. Meanwhile, melt butter in a saucepan. Stir in the flour until smooth. Gradually add milk. Bring to a boil; cook and stir for 2 minutes or until thickened. Stir in Parmesan cheese until melted; set aside. Drain manicotti; set aside.

In a skillet, cook the sausage over medium heat until no longer pink; drain. Add the chicken, spinach, eggs, mozzarella cheese and 3/4 cup white sauce. Stuff into manicotti shells.

Spread 1/2 cup spaghetti sauce each in two ungreased 13-in. x 9-in. x 2-in. baking dishes. Top with manicotti. Pour remaining spaghetti sauce over the top. Reheat the remaining white sauce, stirring constantly. Pour over spaghetti sauce. Bake, uncovered, at 350° for 45-50 minutes. Sprinkle with parsley. **Yield:** 14-16 servings.

Mexican Manicotti

Lisa Bloss, Pawnee City, Nebraska

My family loves both pasta dishes and Mexican food, so I came up with this recipe that combines the best of both worlds. I'm sure you'll find this irresistible, too.

1-1/2 pounds bulk pork sausage
1/2 cup chopped onion
1 can (16 ounces) refried beans
1/2 teaspoon chili powder
1/2 teaspoon ground cumin
1 package (8 ounces) manicotti, cooked and drained
1 can (15 ounces) tomato sauce
1 can (4 ounces) chopped green chilies, optional
2 cups (8 ounces) shredded cheddar cheese

In a skillet, cook sausage and onion until sausage is no longer pink and onion is tender; drain. Stir in beans, chili powder and cumin. Stuff into manicotti shells; place in a greased 13-in. x 9-in. x 2-in. baking dish.

Combine tomato sauce and chilies if desired; pour over manicotti. Sprinkle with cheese. Bake, uncovered, at 350° for 45 minutes or until heated through. **Yield:** 6 servings.

Tuna-Stuffed Jumbo Shells

(Pictured at left)

Phy Bresse, Lumberton, North Carolina

These light, fresh-tasting stuffed shells really star as part of a luncheon menu. I came up with this distinctive combination of ingredients by accident one day using leftovers.

10 jumbo pasta shells
1/2 cup mayonnaise
2 tablespoons sugar
1 can (12 ounces) tuna, drained
1 cup diced celery
1/2 cup diced green onions
1/2 cup diced green pepper
1/2 cup shredded carrot
2 tablespoons minced fresh parsley

CREAMY CELERY DRESSING:

1/4 cup sour cream
1/4 cup sugar
1/4 cup cider vinegar
2 tablespoons mayonnaise
1 teaspoon celery seed
1 teaspoon onion powder
Lettuce leaves and red onion rings, optional

Cook pasta according to package directions; rinse in cold water and drain. In a bowl, combine mayonnaise and sugar. Stir in tuna, celery, onions, green pepper, carrot and parsley. Spoon into pasta shells; cover and refrigerate.

For the dressing, combine sour cream, sugar, vinegar, mayonnaise, celery seed and onion

Pasta Pots

Always cook pasta in a large kettle or Dutch oven to cook it more evenly, prevent it from sticking and avoid boil-overs. Unless you have a very large kettle, don't cook more than 2 pounds of pasta at a time.

If you don't have a pasta pot with a removable liner basket, use a colander or large strainer inside a pot of boiling water in which to cook pasta. That way, you can simply lift the basket out and shake it to drain off excess water.

powder. Arrange lettuce, onion rings and shells on a serving platter; drizzle with dressing. **Yield:** 5 servings.

Manicotti for Two

(Pictured on page 38)

Taste of Home Test Kitchen

We filled manicotti shells with a three-cheese mixture then topped them with store-bought spaghetti sauce beefed up with sausage.

- **4 uncooked manicotti shells**
- **1/2 pound bulk Italian sausage**
- **1-1/2 cups meatless spaghetti sauce**
- **1 cup ricotta cheese**
- **1/2 cup shredded mozzarella cheese, *divided***
- **1/4 cup grated Parmesan cheese**
- **1/2 teaspoon Italian seasoning**
- **1/4 teaspoon garlic powder**
- **1/4 teaspoon pepper**

Cook manicotti according to package directions. Meanwhile, in a skillet, cook the sausage over medium heat until no longer pink; drain. Stir in spaghetti sauce.

Drain manicotti and rinse with cold water. In a bowl, combine the ricotta cheese, 1/4 cup of mozzarella cheese, Parmesan cheese, Italian seasoning, garlic powder and pepper. Carefully stuff manicotti. Place in a greased 11-in. x 7-in. x 2-in. baking dish. Top with sausage mixture.

Bake, uncovered, at 350° for 30-35 minutes or until heated through. Sprinkle with remaining mozzarella. Bake 3-5 minutes longer or until cheese is melted. **Yield:** 2 servings.

Mexican Chicken Manicotti

(Pictured at right)

Keely Jankunas, Corvallis, Montana

Our family enjoys trying different ethnic cuisines. This Italian specialty has a little Mexican zip.

- **1 package (8 ounces) manicotti shells**
- **2 cups cubed cooked chicken**
- **2 cups (8 ounces) shredded Monterey Jack cheese, *divided***
- **1-1/2 cups (6 ounces) shredded cheddar cheese**
- **1 cup (8 ounces) sour cream**
- **1 small onion, diced, *divided***
- **1 can (4 ounces) chopped green chilies, divided**
- **1 can (10-3/4 ounces) condensed cream of chicken soup, undiluted**
- **1 cup salsa**
- **2/3 cup milk**

Cook manicotti according to package directions. Meanwhile, in a large bowl, combine the chicken, 1-1/2 cups Monterey Jack cheese, cheddar cheese, sour cream, half of the onion and 6 tablespoons chilies. In another bowl, combine the soup, salsa, milk, and remaining onion and chilies. Spread 1/2 cup in a greased 13-in. x 9-in. x 2-in. baking dish.

Drain manicotti; stuff each with about 1/4 cup chicken mixture. Arrange over sauce in baking dish. Pour remaining sauce over shells.

Cover and bake at 350° for 30 minutes. Uncover; sprinkle with remaining Monterey Jack cheese. Bake 10 minutes longer or until cheese is melted. **Yield:** 7 servings.

Sausage Broccoli Manicotti

(Pictured below)

Jason Jost, Manitowoc, Wisconsin

Even kids will gobble up their broccoli when it's served this way. I dress up spaghetti sauce with Italian sausage and garlic, then drizzle it over shells stuffed with broccoli and cheese.

- **1 package (8 ounces) manicotti shells**
- **2 cups (16 ounces) small-curd cottage cheese**
- **1 package (10 ounces) frozen chopped broccoli, thawed and well drained**
- **1-1/2 cups (6 ounces) shredded mozzarella cheese, *divided***
- **3/4 cup shredded Parmesan cheese, *divided***
- **1 egg**
- **2 teaspoons minced fresh parsley**
- **1/2 teaspoon onion powder**
- **1/2 teaspoon pepper**

- **1/8 teaspoon garlic powder**
- **1 pound bulk Italian sausage**
- **4 cups meatless spaghetti sauce**
- **2 garlic cloves, minced**

Cook manicotti shells according to package directions. Meanwhile, in a large bowl, combine the cottage cheese, broccoli, 1 cup mozzarella cheese, 1/4 cup Parmesan cheese, egg, parsley, onion powder, pepper and garlic powder. Set aside.

In a skillet, cook sausage over medium heat until no longer pink; drain. Add spaghetti sauce and garlic. Spread 1 cup meat sauce in a greased 13-in. x 9-in. x 2-in. baking dish. Rinse and drain shells; stuff with broccoli mixture. Arrange over sauce. Top with remaining sauce. Sprinkle with remaining mozzarella and Parmesan. Bake, uncovered, at 350° for 40-50 minutes or until heated through. **Yield:** 6-8 servings.

Turkey Manicotti

Whitney Nelson-Smith, Sugar Land, Texas

This is an impressive main course that's easy to make. It's one of my favorites since it uses ground turkey and garlic.

- **2 slices bread**
- **1-1/2 pounds ground turkey**
- **1/4 cup chopped onion**
- **2 garlic cloves, minced**
- **1/2 teaspoon salt**
- **1/4 teaspoon pepper**
- **1 cup (4 ounces) shredded mozzarella cheese**
- **1/2 cup grated Parmesan cheese**
- **14 manicotti shells (8 ounces), cooked and drained**
- **1 jar (30 ounces) spaghetti sauce**

Soak bread in water; squeeze to remove excess water. Tear into small pieces; set aside. In a skillet, cook the turkey, onion, garlic, salt and pepper until meat is no longer pink and onion is tender; drain. Stir in the bread and cheeses; mix well. Spoon into manicotti shells.

Pour half of spaghetti sauce into a greased 13-in. x 9-in. x 2-in. baking dish. Arrange shells over sauce; top with remaining sauce. Cover and bake at 350° for 25-30 minutes or until heated through. **Yield:** 6-8 servings.

Cheesy Chicken Manicotti

Gale Sparling, Pembroke, Ontario

To stuff the shells, I cut off the end of a disposable cake-decorating bag and slip the filling inside. It works like a charm. No mess!

8 manicotti shells
1 can (10-3/4 ounces) condensed tomato soup, undiluted
1/2 cup half-and-half cream
1/2 cup sour cream
1/2 cup water
2 tablespoons mayonnaise
1 to 2 tablespoons grated Parmesan cheese

FILLING:

1 egg
3 cups (12 ounces) shredded mozzarella cheese, *divided*
2 cups cubed cooked chicken
1/2 cup small-curd cottage cheese
1 to 2 tablespoons grated Parmesan cheese
1/8 teaspoon pepper
1 tablespoon minced chives, optional

Cook manicotti according to package directions. Meanwhile, in a bowl, combine the soup, cream, sour cream, water, mayonnaise and Parmesan cheese. Spread about 3/4 cup into a greased 11-in. x 7-in. x 2-in. baking dish. In another bowl, combine the egg, 1 cup of mozzarella cheese, chicken, cottage cheese, Parmesan cheese and pepper.

Drain manicotti shells; stuff each with about 1/3 cup of chicken mixture. Arrange over sauce. Pour remaining sauce over the shells. Top with the remaining mozzarella cheese. Sprinkle with chives if desired. Bake, uncovered, at 350° for 40-45 minutes or until heated through and bubbly. **Yield:** 4 servings.

Editor's Note: Reduced-fat or fat-free mayonnaise may not be substituted for regular mayonnaise in this recipe.

Taco-Filled Pasta Shells

Marge Hodel, Roanoke, Illinois

I've been stuffing pasta shells with different fillings for years, but my family enjoys this version with taco-seasoned meat the most. The frozen shells are so convenient, because you can take out only the number you need for a single-serving lunch or family dinner. Just add zippy taco sauce and bake.

2 pounds ground beef
2 envelopes taco seasoning
1 package (8 ounces) cream cheese, cubed
24 uncooked jumbo pasta shells
1/4 cup butter, melted

ADDITIONAL INGREDIENTS (for each casserole):

1 cup salsa
1 cup taco sauce
1 cup (4 ounces) shredded cheddar cheese
1 cup (4 ounces) shredded Monterey Jack *or* mozzarella cheese
1-1/2 cups crushed tortilla chips
1 cup (8 ounces) sour cream
3 green onions, chopped

In a skillet, cook beef until no longer pink; drain. Add taco seasoning; prepare according to package directions. Add cream cheese; cover and simmer for 5-10 minutes or until melted. Transfer to a bowl; chill for 1 hour. Cook pasta according to package directions; drain. Gently toss with butter. Fill each shell with about 3 tablespoons meat mixture.

Place 12 shells in a greased 9-in. square baking dish. Cover and freeze for up to 3 months. To prepare remaining shells, spoon salsa into a greased 9-in. square baking dish. Top with stuffed shells and taco sauce. Cover and bake at 350° for 30 minutes. Uncover; sprinkle with cheeses and chips. Bake 15 minutes longer or until heated through. Serve with sour cream and onions.

To use frozen shells: Thaw in the refrigerator for 24 hours (shells will be partially frozen). Remove from dish. Add salsa to dish; top with shells and taco sauce. Cover and bake at 350° for 40 minutes. Uncover; continue as above. **Yield:** 2 casseroles (6 servings each).

Manicotti with Eggplant Sauce

(Pictured above)

Barbara Nowakowski
North Tonawanda, New York

This dish has a hearty spinach and cheese filling and a well-seasoned tomato-eggplant sauce.

1 small eggplant, peeled and coarsely chopped
1/2 cup chopped onion
2 garlic cloves, minced
1/2 teaspoon dried tarragon
1/4 teaspoon dried thyme
1 can (14-1/2 ounces) diced tomatoes, undrained
1 can (8 ounces) tomato sauce
1 package (10 ounces) frozen chopped spinach, thawed and well drained
1 cup ricotta cheese
1 cup (4 ounces) shredded mozzarella cheese, *divided*
2 eggs, lightly beaten
1/4 cup grated Parmesan cheese
2 tablespoons minced fresh parsley
6 manicotti shells, cooked, rinsed and drained

In a large skillet coated with nonstick cooking spray, cook and stir the eggplant, onion, garlic, tarragon and thyme until vegetables are tender. Add tomatoes and tomato sauce; bring to a boil. Reduce heat; simmer, uncovered, for 3-4 minutes. Set aside.

In a large bowl, combine spinach, ricotta, 1/2 cup mozzarella, eggs, Parmesan and parsley; mix well. Stuff into shells. Place in an 11-in. x 7-in. x 2-in. baking dish coated with nonstick cooking spray. Spoon eggplant sauce over manicotti; sprinkle with remaining mozzarella. Cover and bake at 350° for 25-30 minutes or until heated through. **Yield:** 6 servings.

Stuffed Pasta Shells

Judy Memo, New Castle, Pennsylvania

This is a different way to use up leftovers. Pasta shells are filled with stuffing and chicken, then topped with an easy sauce.

1-1/2 cups cooked stuffing
2 cups diced cooked chicken *or* turkey
1/2 cup frozen peas, thawed
1/2 cup mayonnaise
18 jumbo pasta shells, cooked and drained
1 can (10-3/4 ounces) condensed cream of chicken soup, undiluted
2/3 cup water
Paprika

Combine the stuffing, chicken, peas and mayonnaise; spoon into pasta shells. Place in a greased 13-in. x 9-in. x 2-in. baking dish. Combine soup and water; pour over shells. Sprinkle with paprika. Cover and bake at 350° for 30 minutes or until heated through. **Yield:** 6 servings.

Stuffed Shells With Meat Sauce

Sunny Folding, Blair, Nebraska

Even my "meat-and-potatoes" husband often requests these filling and flavorful shells.

- **28 jumbo pasta shells**
- **1 pound ground beef**
- **1/2 cup chopped onion**
- **1 garlic clove, minced**
- **1 can (29 ounces) tomato sauce**
- **1 can (28 ounces) Italian diced tomatoes, well drained**
- **1-1/2 teaspoons dried oregano, *divided***
- **1/2 teaspoon dried basil**
- **2 eggs, lightly beaten**
- **3 cups (24 ounces) small-curd cottage cheese**
- **2 packages (10 ounces *each*) frozen chopped spinach, thawed and squeezed dry**
- **2 cups (8 ounces) shredded mozzarella cheese**
- **1/2 cup grated Parmesan cheese**
- **1/2 teaspoon seasoned salt**

Cook pasta shells according to package directions. Meanwhile, in a skillet, cook the beef, onion and garlic over medium heat until meat is no longer pink; drain. Stir in the tomato sauce, tomatoes, 1/2 teaspoon oregano and basil. Bring to a boil. Reduce heat; simmer, uncovered, for 10-15 minutes.

In a large bowl, combine eggs, cottage cheese, spinach, mozzarella, Parmesan, seasoned salt and remaining oregano. Drain pasta shells; cool slightly. Stuff with cheese mixture.

Spread 1 cup of meat sauce into each of two greased 11-in. x 7-in. x 2-in. baking dishes; arrange shells over sauce in a single layer. Pour remaining meat sauce over the shells. Cover and bake at 350° for 40-50 minutes or until a thermometer reads 160°. **Yield:** 6-8 servings.

Enchilada Stuffed Shells

(Pictured at right)

Rebecca Stout, Conroe, Texas

I served this entree to my husband, my sister and her husband, and received many compliments. My brother-in-law is a hard-to-please eater, so when he said he loved it, I was thrilled. He even took leftovers for lunch the next day.

- **15 uncooked jumbo pasta shells**
- **1 pound lean ground turkey**
- **1 can (10 ounces) enchilada sauce**
- **1/2 teaspoon dried minced onion**
- **1/4 teaspoon dried basil**
- **1/4 teaspoon dried oregano**
- **1/4 teaspoon ground cumin**
- **1/2 cup refried beans**
- **1 cup (4 ounces) shredded cheddar cheese**

Cook pasta according to package directions; drain. In a nonstick skillet, cook turkey over medium heat until no longer pink; drain. Stir in enchilada sauce and seasonings; set aside.

Place a rounded teaspoonful of refried beans in each pasta shell, then fill with turkey mixture. Place in an 11-in. x 7-in. x 2-in. baking dish coated with nonstick cooking spray.

Cover and bake at 350° for 25 minutes. Uncover and sprinkle with cheese. Bake 5 minutes longer or until the cheese is melted. **Yield:** 5 servings.

Sage
Parsley
Bay
Sweet Basil
Lemon Balm
Lasagna

Spinach Lasagna Roll-Ups (p. 56)

Bacon 'n' Egg Lasagna

(Pictured above)

Dianne Meyer, Graniteville, Vermont

My sister-in-law served this special dish for Easter breakfast one year, and our whole family loved the mix of bacon, eggs, noodles and cheese. Now I sometimes assemble it the night before and bake it in the morning for a terrific hassle-free brunch entree.

1 pound sliced bacon, diced
1 large onion, chopped
1/3 cup all-purpose flour
1/2 to 1 teaspoon salt
1/4 teaspoon pepper
4 cups milk
12 lasagna noodles, cooked and drained
12 hard-cooked eggs, sliced
2 cups (8 ounces) shredded Swiss cheese
1/3 cup grated Parmesan cheese
2 tablespoons minced fresh parsley

In a skillet, cook bacon until crisp. Remove with a slotted spoon to paper towels. Drain, reserving 1/3 cup drippings. In the drippings, saute onion until tender. Stir in flour, salt and pepper until blended. Gradually stir in milk. Bring to a boil; cook and stir for 2 minutes. Remove from the heat.

Spread 1/2 cup white sauce in a greased 13-in. x 9-in. x 2-in. baking dish. Layer with four noodles, a third of the eggs and bacon, Swiss cheese and sauce. Repeat layers twice. Sprinkle with Parmesan cheese.

Bake, uncovered, at 350° for 35-40 minutes or until bubbly. Sprinkle with parsley. Let stand for 10-15 minutes before cutting. **Yield:** 12 servings.

Cheesy Tuna Lasagna

Virginia Ferris, Lyons, Michigan

This wonderful casserole was added to my recipe collection many years ago, and I've shared it with many others. The tuna and three-cheese blend wins over doubters who say they aren't normally fond of fish.

1 medium onion, chopped
2 tablespoons butter
1 can (12 ounces) tuna, drained and flaked
1 can (10-3/4 ounces) condensed cream of mushroom soup, undiluted
1/2 cup milk
1/2 teaspoon garlic salt
1/2 teaspoon dried oregano
1/4 teaspoon pepper
9 lasagna noodles, cooked and drained
1-1/2 cups (12 ounces) small-curd cottage cheese
8 ounces sliced mozzarella cheese
1/4 cup grated Parmesan cheese

In a large saucepan, saute onion in butter until tender. Stir in the tuna, soup, milk, garlic salt, oregano and pepper until combined.

Spread 3/4 cupful into a greased 11-in. x 7-in. x 2-in. baking dish. Layer with three noodles (trimming if necessary), 3/4 cup tuna mixture, half of the cottage cheese and a third of the mozzarella cheese. Repeat layers. Top with remaining noodles, tuna mixture and mozzarel-

Versatile Lasagna

Lasagna is a popular Italian baked dish made from layering lasagna noodles, meat, cheese and tomato sauce. It's also very flexible.

Try adding a pound of cooked veal, chicken, ground pork or ground beef to the sauce.

Make vegetarian lasagna by chopping leftover vegetables and adding them to the sauce.

Add or subtract cheeses to taste. You can even use cottage cheese or cheddar cheese.

Garnish lasagna with finely chopped Italian parsley. (Italian parsley has flat leaves, rather than curly ones, and has a stronger flavor than regular parsley.)

la. Sprinkle with Parmesan cheese.

Bake, uncovered, at 350° for 25-30 minutes or until bubbly. Let stand for 10-15 minutes before cutting. **Yield:** 6-8 servings.

German Lasagna

(Pictured at right)

Naomi Hochstetler, Woodburn, Indiana

Sausage and sauerkraut are a palate-pleasing pair, especially in lasagna. My family was a little skeptical when I first served this unusual dish. But in no time, they were clamoring for second helpings.

- **3/4 cup butter**
- **3/4 cup all-purpose flour**
- **1 tablespoon beef bouillon granules**
- **2 teaspoons onion salt**
- **2 teaspoons pepper, *divided***
- **1/2 teaspoon white pepper, optional**
- **2-1/4 cups milk**
- **1 can (14-1/2 ounces) chicken broth**
- **1 pound smoked kielbasa *or* Polish sausage, chopped**
- **2 eggs**
- **1-1/2 cups (12 ounces) small-curd cottage cheese**
- **9 lasagna noodles, cooked and drained**
- **1 jar (16 ounces) sauerkraut, rinsed and squeezed dry**
- **2 cups (8 ounces) shredded Monterey Jack cheese, *divided***

In a saucepan, melt butter. Stir in flour, bouillon, onion salt, 1 teaspoon pepper and white pepper if desired until smooth. Gradually stir in milk and broth. Bring to a boil; cook and stir for 2 minutes or until thickened. Add sausage; heat through. Combine eggs, cottage cheese and remaining pepper.

Spread 1 cup sausage mixture in a greased 13-in. x 9-in. x 2-in. baking dish. Layer with three noodles, a third of the sausage mixture, half of the cottage cheese mixture and sauerkraut and 3/4 cup Monterey Jack. Repeat layers. Top with the remaining noodles and sausage mixture (dish will be full).

Cover and bake at 350° for 50-60 minutes or until bubbly. Sprinkle with remaining Monterey Jack. Bake 5 minutes longer or until cheese is melted. Let stand for 10-15 minutes before cutting. **Yield:** 12 servings.

Traditional Lasagna

(Pictured below)

Lorri Foockle, Granville, Illinois

My family first tasted this rich, classic lasagna at a friend's home on Christmas Eve. We were so impressed that it became our own holiday tradition as well. It's requested often by my sister's Italian in-laws—I consider that the highest compliment!

- **1 pound ground beef**
- **3/4 pound bulk pork sausage**
- **3 cans (8 ounces *each*) tomato sauce**
- **2 cans (6 ounces *each*) tomato paste**
- **2 garlic cloves, minced**
- **2 teaspoons sugar**
- **1 teaspoon Italian seasoning**
- **1 teaspoon salt**
- **1/2 teaspoon pepper**
- **3 eggs**
- **3 tablespoons minced fresh parsley**
- **3 cups (24 ounces) small-curd cottage cheese**
- **1 carton (8 ounces) ricotta cheese**
- **1/2 cup grated Parmesan cheese**
- **9 lasagna noodles, cooked and drained**
- **6 slices provolone cheese**
- **3 cups (12 ounces) shredded mozzarella cheese, *divided***

In a skillet, cook beef and sausage over medium heat until no longer pink; drain. Add the next seven ingredients. Simmer, uncovered, for 1 hour, stirring occasionally. In a bowl, combine the eggs, parsley, cottage cheese, ricotta and Parmesan.

Spread 1 cup of meat sauce in an ungreased 13-in. x 9-in. x 2-in. baking dish. Layer with three noodles, provolone cheese, 2 cups cottage cheese mixture, 1 cup mozzarella, three noodles, 2 cups meat sauce, remaining cottage cheese mixture and 1 cup mozzarella. Top with the remaining noodles, meat sauce and mozzarella (dish will be full).

Cover and bake at 375° for 50 minutes. Uncover; bake 20 minutes longer. Let stand for 10-15 minutes before cutting. **Yield:** 12 servings.

Chicken Lasagna Rolls

Darlene Markel, Salem, Oregon

I take pasta to new heights with this clever creation. I roll a cheesy mixture of chicken and broccoli into lasagna noodles, making enough for two dinners. It's nice to have a pan of these roll-ups in the freezer for unexpected company.

- **1 small onion, chopped**
- **3 tablespoons butter**
- **3 tablespoons all-purpose flour**
- **1 can (14-1/2 ounces) chicken broth**
- **1 cup milk**
- **1-1/2 cups (6 ounces) shredded Monterey Jack cheese**
- **3 cups diced cooked chicken**
- **2 packages (10 ounces *each*) frozen chopped broccoli, thawed and drained**
- **2 eggs, beaten**
- **3/4 cup dry bread crumbs**
- **1 jar (6-1/2 ounces) diced pimientos, drained**
- **1/4 cup minced fresh parsley**

1/2 teaspoon salt
12 lasagna noodles, cooked and drained

In a saucepan, saute onion in butter until tender. Stir in flour until blended. Gradually add broth and milk. Bring to a boil; cook and stir for 2 minutes. Remove from the heat; stir in cheese. Pour 1/3 cup each into two greased 8-in. square baking dishes; set aside.

In a bowl, combine 1 cup cheese sauce, chicken, broccoli, eggs, bread crumbs, pimientos, parsley and salt. Spread about 1/2 cup over each noodle. Roll up jelly-roll style, beginning with a short side; secure ends with toothpicks. Place six roll-ups curly end down in each baking dish. Top with remaining cheese sauce.

Cover and freeze one casserole for up to 3 months. Cover and bake second casserole at 350° for 40 minutes. Uncover; bake 5 minutes longer. Discard the toothpicks before serving. **Yield:** 2 casseroles (3 servings each).

To use frozen casserole: Cover and bake at 350° for 1-1/4 hours. Uncover; bake 5 minutes longer or until heated through.

Very Veggie Lasagna

(Pictured above right)

Berniece Baldwin, Glennie, Michigan

I concocted this quick and easy recipe to use up some of the abundant fresh produce from my garden. When I made a batch to share at a church potluck, it received lots of praise.

2 medium carrots, julienned
1 medium zucchini, cut into 1/4-inch slices
1 yellow summer squash, cut into 1/4-inch slices
1 medium onion, sliced
1 cup broccoli florets
1/2 cup sliced celery
1/2 cup julienned sweet red pepper
1/2 cup julienned green pepper
2 garlic cloves, minced
1 teaspoon salt
2 tablespoons vegetable oil
1 jar (28 ounces) spaghetti sauce
14 lasagna noodles, cooked and drained
4 cups (16 ounces) shredded mozzarella cheese

In a large skillet, stir-fry the vegetables, garlic and salt in oil until crisp-tender.

Spread 3/4 cup spaghetti sauce in a greased 13-in. x 9-in. x 2-in. baking dish. Arrange seven noodles over sauce, overlapping as needed. Layer with half of the vegetables, spaghetti sauce and cheese. Repeat layers.

Cover and bake at 350° for 60-65 minutes or until bubbly. Let stand for 15 minutes before cutting. **Yield:** 12 servings.

Draining Lasagna Noodles

To keep lasagna from becoming watery when baking, it's important to drain the noodles well after cooking them. Here's a good way to do that:

Drain and rinse the cooked noodles in a colander. Take each noodle, shake off excess water and lay flat on pieces of waxed paper until most of the water has evaporated.

Creamy Beef Lasagna

(Pictured below)

Jane Frawley, Charles Town, West Virginia

The creamy Stroganoff-like filling in this distinctive lasagna makes it a stick-to-your-ribs entree. My family loves the delicious taste.

1-1/2 pounds ground beef
2 cans (15 ounces *each*) tomato sauce
1/4 cup chopped onion
2 teaspoons sugar
2 teaspoons salt
2 teaspoons Worcestershire sauce
1/2 teaspoon garlic salt
2 packages (8 ounces *each*) cream cheese, softened
1 cup (8 ounces) sour cream
1/4 cup milk
18 lasagna noodles, cooked and drained
1 cup (4 ounces) shredded cheddar cheese
Minced fresh parsley, optional

In a skillet, cook beef over medium heat until no longer pink; drain. Stir in tomato sauce, onion, sugar, salt, Worcestershire sauce and garlic salt. In a mixing bowl, beat cream cheese, sour cream and milk until smooth.

In a greased 13-in. x 9-in. x 2-in. baking dish, layer a fourth of the meat sauce, six noodles and a third of cream cheese mixture. Repeat layers twice. Top with remaining meat sauce.

Cover and bake at 350° for 40 minutes. Uncover; sprinkle with cheddar cheese. Bake 5 minutes longer or until cheese is melted. Let stand for 10-15 minutes before cutting. Sprinkle with parsley. **Yield:** 12 servings.

Pepperoni Lasagna

Barbara McIntosh, Midland, Texas

I've served this lasagna for years. When our children were small, they preferred it more than a steak dinner! Now my grandchildren request that I bring a pan along when I visit.

1-1/2 pounds ground beef
1 small onion, chopped
2-1/2 cups water
1 can (8 ounces) tomato sauce
1 can (6 ounces) tomato paste
1 teaspoon beef bouillon granules
1 tablespoon dried parsley flakes
2 teaspoons Italian seasoning
1 teaspoon salt
1/4 teaspoon garlic salt
2 eggs
1-1/2 cups (12 ounces) small-curd cottage cheese
1/2 cup sour cream
8 lasagna noodles, cooked and drained
1 package (3-1/2 ounces) sliced pepperoni
2 cups (8 ounces) shredded mozzarella cheese
1/2 cup grated Parmesan cheese

In a skillet, cook beef and onion over medium heat until meat is no longer pink; drain. Add water, tomato sauce, tomato paste, bouillon and seasonings. Bring to a boil. Reduce heat; simmer, uncovered, for 30 minutes. In a bowl, combine eggs, cottage cheese and sour cream.

Spread 1/2 cup meat sauce into a greased 13-in. x 9-in. x 2-in. baking dish. Layer with four noodles, the cottage cheese mixture and pepperoni. Top with remaining noodles and meat sauce. Sprinkle with mozzarella and Parmesan cheeses.

Cover and bake at 350° for 35 minutes. Uncover; bake 10 minutes longer or until heated through. Let stand for 10-15 minutes before cutting. **Yield:** 12 servings.

Turkey Ravioli Lasagna

(Pictured at right)

Anne Plesmid, Sagamore Hills, Ohio

I came up with this "shortcut" lasagna one day when the dinner hour was fast approaching and all I had in the freezer was some frozen ravioli. Now I make it often.

1 pound ground turkey *or* beef
1/2 teaspoon garlic powder
Salt and pepper to taste
1 cup grated carrots
1 cup sliced fresh mushrooms
1 tablespoon olive oil
1 jar (28 ounces) spaghetti sauce
1 package (25 ounces) frozen cheese ravioli, cooked and drained
3 cups (12 ounces) shredded mozzarella cheese
1/2 cup grated Parmesan cheese
Minced fresh parsley

In a skillet, cook turkey over medium heat until no longer pink; drain. Sprinkle with garlic powder, salt and pepper; set aside. In a saucepan, cook carrots and mushrooms in oil until tender. Stir in the spaghetti sauce.

Spread 1/2 cup sauce in a greased 13-in. x 9-in. x 2-in. baking dish. Layer with half of the ravioli, spaghetti sauce mixture, turkey and cheeses. Repeat the layers and sprinkle with parsley.

Cover and bake at 375° for 25-30 minutes or until bubbly. Uncover; bake 10 minutes longer. Let stand for 10-15 minutes before cutting. **Yield:** 12 servings.

Lazy Lasagna

Carol Mead, Los Alamos, New Mexico

Lasagna may seem like more work than it's worth for two people. But one day when I had a craving for it, I devised a simple recipe and called it Lazy Lasagna.

1 cup spaghetti sauce
1/2 cup cottage cheese
3/4 cup shredded mozzarella cheese
1-1/2 cups cooked wide egg noodles
2 tablespoons grated Parmesan cheese

Warm the spaghetti sauce; stir in cottage cheese and mozzarella. Fold in noodles. Pour into two greased 2-cup casseroles. Sprinkle with Parmesan cheese. Bake, uncovered, at 375° for 20 minutes or until bubbly. **Yield:** 2 servings.

Meatball Lasagna

(Pictured above)

Addella Thomas, Mt. Sterling, Illinois

I crumble leftover meatballs into the homemade spaghetti sauce I use in this cheesy lasagna.

2 cans (14-1/2 ounces *each*) diced tomatoes, undrained
1 can (8 ounces) tomato sauce
1 cup water
1 can (6 ounces) tomato paste
1 medium onion, chopped
1 garlic clove, minced
1 tablespoon dried basil
4 teaspoons dried parsley flakes
2 teaspoons sugar
Garlic salt to taste
8 uncooked lasagna noodles
24 cooked meatballs
1 egg
1 cup ricotta cheese
2 cups (8 ounces) shredded mozzarella cheese
3/4 cup grated Parmesan cheese

In a large saucepan, combine the first 10 ingredients. Bring to a boil. Reduce heat; cover and simmer for 20 minutes. Meanwhile, cook lasagna noodles according to package directions; drain. Crumble meatballs into the sauce.

In a small bowl, combine egg and ricotta cheese. Spoon 1 cup of the meat sauce into a greased 13-in. x 9-in. x 2-in. baking dish. Layer with half of the noodles, ricotta mixture, meat sauce, mozzarella and Parmesan cheeses. Repeat layers. Cover and bake at 350° for 45 minutes. Uncover; bake 5-10 minutes longer or until golden brown. Let stand for 15 minutes before cutting. **Yield:** 8-10 servings.

Lasagna Con Carne

Mary Lou Wills, La Plata, Maryland

This dish is sort of like chili in a pan. I came up with the recipe one day using just ingredients I had on hand. It was an instant hit.

1 pound ground beef
1 jar (16 ounces) salsa
1 can (16 ounces) kidney beans, rinsed and drained
1 can (14-3/4 ounces) cream-style corn
1 large onion, chopped
3/4 cup chopped green pepper
1 celery rib, chopped
1 tablespoon minced fresh basil *or* 1 teaspoon dried basil
1 teaspoon salt
1 teaspoon chili powder
3 garlic cloves, minced
12 lasagna noodles, cooked and drained
2 cups (8 ounces) shredded mozzarella cheese
1/2 cup grated Parmesan cheese

In a large skillet, cook beef over medium heat until no longer pink; drain. Add salsa, beans, vegetables and seasonings. Reduce heat; cover and simmer for 15 minutes.

Spread a fourth of meat sauce in a greased 13-in. x 9-in. x 2-in. baking dish; top with four noodles. Repeat once. Top with half of remaining sauce and half of cheeses. Layer with remaining noodles, sauce and cheeses.

Cover and bake at 350° for 30 minutes. Uncover; bake 15-20 minutes longer or until heated through. Let stand for 15 minutes before cutting. **Yield:** 12 servings.

Bacon-Colby Lasagna

Cathy McCartney, Davenport, Iowa

With both bacon and ground beef, this hearty dish is a real crowd-pleaser.

2 pounds ground beef
2 medium onions, chopped
2 pounds sliced bacon, cooked and crumbled
2 cans (15 ounces *each*) tomato sauce
2 cans (14-1/2 ounces *each*) diced tomatoes, undrained
2 tablespoons sugar
1 teaspoon salt
24 lasagna noodles, cooked and drained
8 cups (32 ounces) shredded Colby cheese

In a Dutch oven, cook beef and onions over medium heat until meat is no longer pink; drain. Stir in the bacon, tomato sauce, tomatoes, sugar and salt; cook until heated through.

Spread 1 cup meat sauce in each of two greased 13-in. x 9-in. x 2-in. baking dishes. Layer four noodles, 1-2/3 cups meat sauce and 1-1/3 cups cheese in each dish. Repeat layers twice.

Cover and bake at 350° for 40 minutes. Uncover; bake 5-10 minutes longer or until bubbly. Let stand for 15 minutes before cutting. **Yield:** 2 casseroles (12 servings each).

Chicken Cheese Lasagna

(Pictured at right)

Mary Ann Kosmas, Minneapolis, Minnesota

In place of half traditional red-sauce lasagna, make this version with chicken and a white sauce.

1/2 cup butter
1 medium onion, chopped
1 garlic clove, minced
1/2 cup all-purpose flour
1 teaspoon salt
2 cups chicken broth
1-1/2 cups milk
4 cups (16 ounces) shredded mozzarella cheese, *divided*
1 cup grated Parmesan cheese, *divided*
1 teaspoon dried basil
1 teaspoon dried oregano
1/2 teaspoon white pepper
1 carton (15 ounces) ricotta cheese
1 tablespoon minced fresh parsley
9 lasagna noodles (8 ounces), cooked and drained
2 packages (10 ounces *each*) frozen spinach, thawed and well drained
2 cups cubed cooked chicken

In a saucepan, melt butter over medium heat. Saute onion and garlic until tender. Stir in flour and salt; cook until bubbly. Gradually stir in broth and milk. Bring to a boil, stirring constantly. Boil 1 minute. Stir in 2 cups mozzarella, 1/2 cup Parmesan, basil, oregano and pepper; set aside. In a bowl, combine ricotta cheese, parsley and remaining mozzarella; set aside.

Spread one-quarter of the cheese sauce into a greased 13-in. x 9-in. x 2-in. baking dish; cover with one-third of the noodles. Top with half of the ricotta mixture, half of the spinach and half of the chicken. Cover with one-quarter of cheese sauce and one-third of noodles. Repeat layers of ricotta mixture, spinach, chicken and one-quarter cheese sauce. Cover with remaining noodles and cheese sauce. Sprinkle with remaining Parmesan.

Bake, uncovered, at 350° for 35-40 minutes. Let stand 15 minutes before cutting. **Yield:** 12 servings.

Spaghet

Spaghetti Supreme (p. 67)

Mom's Hearty Spaghetti

(Pictured above)

Grace Yaskovic, Branchville, New Jersey

Flavored with Italian sausage and dotted with tender meatballs, the savory from-scratch sauce made this dish one of my mom's most-requested. We five kids were always thrilled to hear it was on the menu.

1 egg
1/4 cup milk
1 cup soft bread crumbs
1/2 teaspoon salt
1/2 teaspoon garlic powder
1/2 teaspoon minced fresh parsley
1 pound ground beef

SAUCE:

1 pound Italian sausage links, cut into 2-inch pieces
1 large onion, chopped
1 medium green pepper, chopped
2 cans (28 ounces *each*) plum *or* whole tomatoes, drained and diced
2 cans (8 ounces *each*) tomato sauce
1 can (14-1/2 ounces) beef broth
1 can (6 ounces) tomato paste
2 garlic cloves, minced
2 teaspoons *each* dried basil, oregano and parsley flakes
2 teaspoons sugar
Salt and pepper to taste
Hot cooked spaghetti
Grated Parmesan cheese

In a bowl, combine the first six ingredients. Crumble beef over mixture and mix well. Shape into eight meatballs. Brown in a Dutch oven over medium heat; drain and set meatballs aside.

In the same pan, cook sausage, onion and green pepper until vegetables are tender; drain. Add the tomatoes, tomato sauce, broth, tomato paste, garlic and seasonings. Add meatballs; stir gently. Bring to a boil.

Reduce heat; cover and simmer for 2-3 hours. Serve over spaghetti; sprinkle with Parmesan cheese. **Yield:** 8 servings.

Swift Spaghetti

Louise Miller, Westminster, Maryland

I add dry onion soup mix to the water when cooking my spaghetti and then stir in a nicely seasoned meat sauce. This dish has so much flavor that I'm always asked for the recipe.

5-1/2 cups water
1 package (7 ounces) spaghetti
1 envelope onion soup mix
1 pound ground beef
1 can (8 ounces) tomato sauce
1 can (6 ounces) tomato paste
1 tablespoon dried parsley flakes
1 teaspoon dried oregano
1/2 teaspoon dried basil
1/4 to 1/2 teaspoon garlic powder

In a large saucepan, bring water to a boil. Add spaghetti and dry soup mix. Cook for 12-15 minutes or until spaghetti is tender (do not drain).

Meanwhile, in a skillet, cook beef over medium heat until no longer pink; drain. Stir in the tomato sauce, tomato paste, parsley, oregano, basil and garlic powder. Add to the spaghetti mixture; heat through. **Yield:** 4-6 servings.

Spinach Pepperoni Spaghetti

Joanne Laing Soyk, Milwaukee, Wisconsin

I use fresh basil to flavor this medley of mushrooms, pepperoni, spinach and spaghetti. It's delicious accompanied by breadsticks.

- **1 package (7 ounces) thin spaghetti**
- **1/2 pound fresh mushrooms, sliced**
- **1 package (3-1/2 ounces) pepperoni, cut into thin strips**
- **2 tablespoons butter**
- **6 cups torn fresh spinach**
- **2 tablespoons minced fresh basil**
- **2 teaspoons lemon juice**
- **4 tablespoons grated Parmesan cheese, *divided***

Cook spaghetti according to package directions. Meanwhile, in a skillet, saute mushrooms and pepperoni in butter until mushrooms are tender. Stir in spinach, basil and lemon juice. Cook and stir for 2 minutes or until spinach is wilted.

Drain spaghetti. Toss with pepperoni mixture and 3 tablespoons Parmesan cheese. Sprinkle with the remaining Parmesan cheese. **Yield:** 4 servings.

Spinach-Beef Spaghetti Pie

(Pictured at right)

Carol Hicks, Pensacola, Florida

With its spaghetti crust, this cheesy ground beef, tomato and spinach pie is always a hit when I serve it. Each neat slice has layers of pasta, cream cheese filling and spinach.

- **6 ounces uncooked thin spaghetti**
- **2 eggs, lightly beaten**
- **1/3 cup grated Parmesan cheese**
- **1 pound ground beef**
- **1/2 cup chopped onion**
- **1/4 cup chopped green pepper**
- **1 jar (14 ounces) meatless spaghetti sauce**
- **1 teaspoon Creole seasoning**
- **3/4 teaspoon garlic powder**
- **1/2 teaspoon dried basil**
- **1/2 teaspoon dried oregano**
- **1 package (8 ounces) cream cheese, softened**
- **1 package (10 ounces) frozen chopped spinach, thawed and squeezed dry**
- **1/2 cup shredded mozzarella cheese**

Cook pasta according to package directions; drain. Add eggs and Parmesan cheese. Press onto the bottom and up the sides of a greased 9-in. deep-dish pie plate. Bake at 350° for 10 minutes.

Meanwhile, in a skillet, cook the beef, onion and green pepper over medium heat until meat is no longer pink; drain. Stir in spaghetti sauce and seasonings. Bring to a boil. Reduce heat; cover and simmer for 10 minutes.

Between two pieces of waxed paper, roll out cream cheese into a 7-in. circle. Place in the crust. Top with spinach and meat sauce. Sprinkle with mozzarella cheese. Bake at 350° for 20-30 minutes or until set. **Yield:** 6-8 servings.

Baked Spaghetti

(Pictured below)

Betty Rabe, Mahtomedi, Minnesota

This satisfying pasta bake is quick to make and pleases young and old alike. Plus, it's a nice change from the more traditional sauce that's simmered on the stove. Add a salad and breadsticks, and you're ready for company.

8 ounces uncooked spaghetti, broken into thirds
1 egg
1/2 cup milk
1/2 teaspoon salt
1/2 pound ground beef
1/2 pound bulk Italian sausage
1 small onion, chopped
1/4 cup chopped green pepper
1 jar (14 ounces) meatless spaghetti sauce
1 can (8 ounces) tomato sauce
1 to 2 cups (4 to 8 ounces) shredded mozzarella cheese

Cook spaghetti according to package directions; drain. In a large bowl, beat the egg, milk and salt. Add spaghetti; toss to coat. Transfer to a greased 13-in. x 9-in. x 2-in. baking dish.

In a large skillet, cook the beef, sausage, onion and green pepper over medium heat until meat is no longer pink; drain. Add spaghetti sauce and tomato sauce; mix well. Spoon over the spaghetti mixture.

Bake, uncovered, at 350° for 20 minutes. Sprinkle with the cheese. Bake 10 minutes longer or until cheese is melted. Let stand for 10 minutes before cutting. **Yield:** 6-8 servings.

Spaghetti Fish Supper

Charolette Westfall, Houston, Texas

This colorful blend of fish, vegetables and pasta in a creamy sauce is so satisfying. I've also substituted cooked chicken for the fish, and it's just as good.

4 green onions, chopped
5 garlic cloves, minced
2 tablespoons olive oil
1 can (14-1/2 ounces) chicken broth
2 tablespoons dried parsley flakes
1/2 teaspoon salt
1/4 teaspoon pepper
1/4 teaspoon ground cumin
2 tablespoons cornstarch
1/2 cup apple juice
1/2 pound fresh *or* frozen orange roughy, haddock *or* red snapper fillets, thawed and cut into 1-inch pieces
1 medium tomato, seeded and chopped
1 cup chopped fresh broccoli florets
8 ounces uncooked thin spaghetti
1/4 cup sliced ripe olives

In a large skillet, saute onions and garlic in oil until tender. Stir in the broth, parsley, salt, pepper and cumin. Cover and simmer for 2 minutes. Combine cornstarch and apple juice until smooth; pour into the skillet. Cook and stir for 1-2 minutes or until thickened.

Stir in the fish, tomato and broccoli. Cover and cook for 2 minutes or until fish easily flakes with a fork.

Meanwhile, cook spaghetti according to package directions; drain and toss with olives. Top with fish mixture. **Yield:** 2 servings.

Spaghetti Supreme

(Pictured on page 62)

Shannon Donnan, Saskatoon, Saskatchewan

When friends and family rave about this skillet supper, I'm almost embarrassed to tell them how easy it is to prepare!

4 bacon strips, diced
1/2 pound ground beef
2 celery ribs, chopped
1 large onion, chopped
1 cup sliced fresh mushrooms
1/2 cup chopped green pepper
1 can (10-3/4 ounces) condensed tomato soup, undiluted
1 teaspoon Worcestershire sauce
1/4 teaspoon salt
Dash pepper
4 ounces spaghetti *or* angel hair pasta, cooked and drained

In a skillet, cook bacon until crisp. Remove with a slotted spoon and set aside. In the drippings, cook the beef, celery, onion, mushrooms and green pepper over medium heat until the meat is no longer pink and the vegetables are tender; drain.

Stir in the soup, Worcestershire sauce, salt, pepper and bacon; mix well. Stir in pasta. Cover and simmer for 20 minutes or until heated through. **Yield:** 4 servings.

Cooking Pasta

For 1 pound of dried pasta, bring 4 to 5 quarts of water to a full rolling boil. Carefully add the pasta all at once and return to a rolling boil, stirring occasionally.

To prevent pasta from sticking, add 1 teaspoon of olive or vegetable oil to the cooking water. Rubbing oil around the top of the pot will also help prevent boilovers.

If desired, you can also give a little flavor to the pasta by adding 1 or 2 tablespoons of salt to the water or throwing in dried herbs and seasonings.

Spaghetti Pork Chops

(Pictured above)

Ellen Gallavan, Midland, Michigan

The moist chops simmer to perfection in a tangy sauce, then are served over pasta. This was one of my mother's most-loved recipes.

3 cans (8 ounces *each*) tomato sauce
1 can (10-3/4 ounces) condensed tomato soup, undiluted
1 small onion, finely chopped
1 bay leaf
1 teaspoon celery seed
1/2 teaspoon Italian seasoning
6 bone-in pork chops (1 inch thick)
2 tablespoons olive oil
Hot cooked spaghetti

In a 5-qt. slow cooker, combine the tomato sauce, soup, onion, bay leaf, celery seed and Italian seasoning. In a large skillet, brown pork chops in oil. Add to the slow cooker.

Cover and cook on low for 6-8 hours or until meat is tender. Discard bay leaf. Serve chops and sauce over spaghetti. **Yield:** 6 servings.

Southwestern Spaghetti

(Pictured above)

Beth Coffee, Hartford City, Indiana

Chili powder and cumin give a mild Mexican flavor to this colorful one-skillet supper with chunks of fresh zucchini.

- **3/4 pound ground beef**
- **2-1/4 cups water**
- **1 can (15 ounces) tomato sauce**
- **2 teaspoons chili powder**
- **1/2 teaspoon garlic powder**
- **1/2 teaspoon salt**
- **1/2 teaspoon ground cumin**
- **1 package (7 ounces) thin spaghetti, broken into thirds**
- **6 small zucchini (about 1 pound), cut into chunks**
- **1/2 cup shredded cheddar cheese**

In a large skillet, cook beef over medium heat until no longer pink; drain. Remove beef and keep warm. In the same skillet, combine the water, tomato sauce, chili powder, garlic powder, salt and cumin; bring to a boil. Stir in spaghetti; return to a boil. Boil for 6 minutes.

Add the zucchini. Cook 4-5 minutes longer or until spaghetti and zucchini are tender, stirring several times. Stir in the beef; sprinkle with cheese. Serve immediately. **Yield:** 5 servings.

Festive Spaghetti 'n' Meatballs

Mary Ann Kosmas, Minneapolis, Minnesota

When I don't have enough time to make spaghetti sauce from scratch, I dress up a store-bought jar with fresh vegetables and frozen meatballs. A touch of wine makes it special.

- **1/2 pound sliced fresh mushrooms**
- **1 large green pepper, julienned**
- **1 large onion, halved and sliced**
- **2 tablespoons olive oil**
- **1/4 cup red wine *or* water**
- **1 jar (26 ounces) meatless spaghetti sauce**
- **1 package (12 ounces) frozen cooked Italian meatballs**
- **1 package (16 ounces) spaghetti**

In a large saucepan, saute the mushrooms, green pepper and onion in oil until crisp-tender; stir in wine or water. Bring to a boil; cook for 2 minutes. Stir in spaghetti sauce and meatballs. Return to a boil. Reduce heat; simmer, uncovered, for 10-15 minutes or until meatballs are heated through.

Meanwhile, cook pasta according to package directions; drain. Serve meatballs and sauce over spaghetti. **Yield:** 6 servings.

Garden-Fresh Spaghetti

Sue Yaeger, Boone, Iowa

This pasta sauce with fresh-from-the-garden flavor is chock-full of peppers, mushrooms, carrots and onion. It makes a big batch, so you'll have plenty to serve over spaghetti with leftovers.

- 4 cups sliced fresh mushrooms
- 3 medium carrots, coarsely chopped
- 1 cup chopped celery
- 1 cup chopped onion
- 1/2 cup chopped green pepper
- 1/2 cup chopped sweet red pepper
- 4 garlic cloves, minced
- 1/4 cup vegetable oil
- 2 cans (28 ounces *each*) crushed tomatoes
- 2 cans (15 ounces *each*) tomato sauce
- 1 can (12 ounces) tomato paste
- 1 cup beef broth
- 2 teaspoons dried basil
- 2 teaspoons dried oregano
- 1-1/2 teaspoons brown sugar
- 1 teaspoon salt
- 1/2 teaspoon pepper
- 1 cup grated Parmesan cheese
- Hot cooked spaghetti

In a Dutch oven, saute the mushrooms, carrots, celery, onion, peppers and garlic in oil until tender. Add the next 10 ingredients. Bring to a boil. Reduce heat; cover and simmer for 1 hour. Serve over spaghetti. **Yield:** 15 cups sauce.

Parsley Pesto Spaghetti

Christine Wilson, Sellersville, Pennsylvania

This is a fun and tasty way to serve traditional pasta. I adapted it from a recipe I came across years ago.

- 1 package (1 pound) spaghetti
- 3 cups packed fresh parsley sprigs
- 1 cup blanched almonds
- 2 to 3 garlic cloves, minced
- 1-1/4 cups grated Parmesan cheese
- 1/2 cup butter, melted
- Salt and pepper to taste

Cook spaghetti according to package directions. Meanwhile, place parsley, almonds and garlic in a food processor or blender; cover and process until finely chopped. Transfer to a large serving bowl; stir in cheese and butter. Drain spaghetti and add to pesto with salt and pepper; toss to coat. **Yield:** 10 servings.

Chicken Spaghetti Toss

(Pictured below)

Cindy Dorband, Monument, Colorado

This is a tempting entree that can easily be increased for larger get-togethers.

- 5 green onions, chopped
- 2 garlic cloves, minced
- 2 tablespoons butter
- 2 tablespoons olive oil
- 1-1/2 pounds boneless skinless chicken breasts, cubed
- 3 tablespoons lemon juice
- 3 tablespoons minced fresh parsley
- 1 teaspoon seasoned salt
- 1/2 teaspoon lemon-pepper seasoning
- 1 package (7 ounces) thin spaghetti

In a large skillet, saute onions and garlic in butter and oil until tender. Stir in the chicken, lemon juice, parsley, seasoned salt and lemon-pepper. Saute for 15-20 minutes or until chicken juices run clear.

Meanwhile, cook spaghetti according to package directions; drain. Add to chicken mixture and toss. **Yield:** 4 servings.

Ham Spaghetti Skillet

(Pictured below)

Edna Shaver, San Antonio, Texas

Here's a satisfying skillet of ham, chicken and spaghetti that's tossed in a creamy sauce. For make-ahead convenience, assemble it in a casserole the day before and store it in the fridge.

6 ounces thin spaghetti, broken into 2-inch pieces
6 green onions, chopped
1 jar (4-1/2 ounces) sliced mushrooms, drained
1/4 cup butter
1-1/2 cups cubed fully cooked ham
1 cup cubed cooked chicken
1 cup (8 ounces) sour cream
1 cup (8 ounces) small-curd cottage cheese
1/2 teaspoon celery salt
1/2 teaspoon salt
1/8 teaspoon pepper
Shredded cheddar cheese

Cook spaghetti according to package directions. Meanwhile, in a large skillet, saute onions and mushrooms in butter until tender; reduce heat to low.

Drain spaghetti. Add the spaghetti, ham, chicken, sour cream, cottage cheese, celery salt, salt and pepper to the skillet. Cook and stir until heated through. Remove from the heat. Sprinkle with cheese. **Yield:** 4 servings.

Turkey Spaghetti Pie

Elnora Johnson, Union City, Tennessee

This pretty spaghetti pie blends well-seasoned ground turkey, cheese, veggies and tomato sauce in a crust formed from spaghetti. It's tasty comfort food your family will request again and again.

1 pound ground turkey breast
1 cup chopped green pepper
1/2 cup chopped onion
1/2 cup tomato sauce
1/2 teaspoon dried basil
1/2 teaspoon fennel seed, crushed
1/8 teaspoon pepper
6 ounces spaghetti
1 egg
1 tablespoon butter, melted
1 tablespoon grated Parmesan cheese
1 teaspoon dried parsley flakes
1/2 cup shredded mozzarella cheese, *divided*

In a large skillet, cook the turkey, green pepper and onion over medium heat until the turkey is no longer pink; drain. Stir in the tomato sauce, basil, fennel seed and pepper. Bring to a boil. Reduce heat; simmer, uncovered, for 20-30 minutes.

Meanwhile, cook the spaghetti according to package directions; drain. In a bowl, combine the spaghetti, egg, butter, Parmesan cheese and parsley flakes. Form a crust in a 9-in. pie plate coated with nonstick cooking spray.

Stir 1/4 cup mozzarella cheese into the turkey

mixture; spoon into spaghetti crust. Cover and bake at 350° for 30 minutes. Uncover and sprinkle with remaining mozzarella cheese. Bake 15 minutes longer or until cheese is melted. Let stand for 10 minutes before cutting into wedges. **Yield:** 6 servings.

Ginger Pork Over Spaghetti

Linda Stone, Dothan, Alabama

I first tasted this speedy skillet dish when my daughter and son-in-law prepared it for us. With a salad and French bread, it makes a wonderful meal.

- **2 pounds ground pork**
- **2 garlic cloves, minced**
- **1/2 teaspoon ground ginger *or* 2 teaspoons minced fresh gingerroot**
- **1/2 teaspoon crushed red pepper flakes**
- **7-1/2 teaspoons cornstarch**
- **2 cups water**
- **1/2 cup soy sauce**
- **1/4 cup white wine *or* chicken broth**
- **1 cup sliced green onions**
- **6 cups hot cooked spaghetti**

In a skillet, cook the pork, garlic, ginger and pepper flakes over medium heat until meat is no longer pink; drain.

In a bowl, combine the cornstarch, water, soy sauce and wine or broth until smooth. Add to pork mixture with onions. Bring to a boil; cook and stir for 2 minutes or until thickened.

Place spaghetti in a large bowl. Add pork mixture and toss to coat. **Yield:** 6-8 servings.

Scallops with Spaghetti

(Pictured above right)

Susan D'Amore, West Chester, Pennsylvania

My mom used to serve this stir-fry when I was young. Now it's one of my own family's most-requested dinners. It tastes great when made with shrimp, too.

- **1 package (7 ounces) spaghetti**
- **1 pound sea scallops**
- **4 garlic cloves, minced**
- **2 tablespoons olive oil**
- **1 tablespoon butter**
- **1-1/2 cups julienned carrots**
- **1-1/2 cups frozen French-style green beans, thawed**
- **1 sweet red pepper, julienned**
- **2 tablespoons lemon juice**
- **1 tablespoon minced fresh parsley**
- **1 tablespoon minced fresh basil *or* 1 teaspoon dried basil**
- **1/4 teaspoon salt**
- **1/8 teaspoon pepper**

Cook spaghetti according to package directions. Meanwhile, in a large skillet or wok, stir-fry scallops and garlic in oil and butter for 5 minutes or until scallops are opaque; remove and keep warm.

In the same skillet, stir-fry the carrots, beans and red pepper until crisp-tender. Stir in the lemon juice, parsley, basil, salt and pepper. Drain spaghetti. Add scallops and spaghetti to the vegetable mixture; toss to coat. **Yield:** 4 servings.

Spaghetti Carbonara

Taste of Home Test Kitchen

Minus the egg and bacon, this makes a great side dish alongside meat or poultry.

- **1 package (8 ounces) spaghetti**
- **1 garlic clove, minced**
- **3 tablespoons butter *or* margarine**
- **1 egg, beaten**
- **8 bacon strips, cooked and crumbled**
- **1/4 cup grated Parmesan cheese**

Cook spaghetti according to package directions. Meanwhile, in a large skillet, saute garlic in butter over medium heat. Reduce heat to low; add egg. Cook and stir until the egg mixture coats a metal spoon and reaches 160° (mixture will look like a soft frothy egg). Drain spaghetti and place in a bowl. Pour sauce over and sprinkle with bacon; toss gently to coat. Gently stir in Parmesan cheese. **Yield:** 4 servings.

Spaghetti with Homemade Turkey Sausage

(Pictured above)

Shirley Goodson, West Allis, Wisconsin

This is a savory, satisfying main dish with rich flavor. The easy-to-make turkey sausage has just the right amount of seasoning.

- **1 pound ground turkey**
- **1 teaspoon fennel seed, crushed**
- **1 teaspoon water**
- **1/2 teaspoon salt**
- **1/2 teaspoon pepper**
- **1 jar (27 ounces) spaghetti sauce**
- **12 ounces spaghetti, cooked and drained**

In a bowl, combine turkey, fennel seed, water, salt and pepper. Refrigerate overnight. Crumble into bite-size pieces; cook in a skillet over medium heat until no pink remains. Add spaghetti sauce and heat through. Serve over hot spaghetti. **Yield:** 6 servings.

Garlic Spaghetti

Jackie Messina, Chardon, Ohio

I make this family favorite at least two or three times a month. It's wonderful with a salad and fresh Italian bread. This meatless main dish is easy on the pocketbook.

- **1 package (16 ounces) spaghetti**
- **10 garlic cloves, minced**
- **1/4 cup olive *or* vegetable oil**
- **1/4 cup minced fresh parsley**
- **2 teaspoons dried oregano *or* 2 tablespoons minced fresh oregano**
- **1 teaspoon salt**
- **1/4 teaspoon pepper**
- **1/2 cup grated Parmesan cheese**

Cook spaghetti according to package directions. Meanwhile, in a skillet over low heat, cook garlic in oil until lightly browned. Remove from the heat; stir in parsley, oregano, salt and pepper. Drain spaghetti; place in a large bowl. Add garlic mixture and Parmesan cheese; toss to coat. **Yield:** 4 servings.

Chili-ghetti

Cindy Cuykendall, Skaneateles, New York

I created this recipe when unexpected guests stopped over and I didn't have enough chili for everyone. I stretched what I had by tossing in cooked spaghetti. The surprisingly simple supper became a family favorite.

1 package (7 ounces) spaghetti
1 pound ground beef
1 small onion, chopped
1 can (16 ounces) kidney beans, rinsed and drained
1 can (14-1/2 ounces) diced tomatoes, undrained
1 can (4 ounces) mushroom stems and pieces, drained
1/3 cup water
1 envelope chili seasoning
2 tablespoons grated Parmesan cheese
1/4 cup shredded mozzarella cheese

Cook spaghetti according to package directions. Meanwhile, in a large skillet, cook beef and onion over medium heat until meat is no longer pink; drain.

Drain spaghetti; add to beef mixture. Stir in the beans, tomatoes, mushrooms, water, chili seasoning and Parmesan cheese. Cover and simmer for 10 minutes. Sprinkle with mozzarella cheese. **Yield:** 8 servings.

Creamy Garden Spaghetti

(Pictured at right)

Karrie Fimbres, Sparks, Nevada

I've always liked the versatility of pasta. This cheesy vegetable noodle dish is one of my grandmother's favorites, so I make it often when we get together.

1/2 pound fresh broccoli, broken into florets
1-1/2 cups sliced zucchini
1-1/2 cups sliced fresh mushrooms
1 large carrot, sliced
1 tablespoon olive oil
8 ounces uncooked spaghetti
1/4 cup chopped onion
3 garlic cloves, minced
2 tablespoons butter
2 tablespoons all-purpose flour
2 teaspoons chicken bouillon granules
1 teaspoon dried thyme
2 cups milk
1/2 cup shredded Swiss cheese
1/2 cup shredded mozzarella cheese

In a large skillet, saute the broccoli, zucchini, mushrooms and carrot in oil until crisp-tender. Remove from the heat and set aside.

Cook spaghetti according to package directions. In another saucepan, saute onion and garlic in butter until tender. Stir in the flour, bouillon and thyme until blended. Gradually add milk. Bring to a boil; cook and stir for 2 minutes or until thickened.

Reduce heat to low; stir in cheeses until melted. Add the vegetables; heat through. Drain spaghetti; toss with vegetable mixture. **Yield:** 4 servings.

Fettuccin
Lingui

Pepper Steak Fettuccine (p.80)

until the vegetables are tender. Add cream, peas, onions, Parmesan, basil, salt, pepper and nutmeg; bring to a boil.

Reduce heat; simmer for 3 minutes, stirring frequently. Rinse and drain linguine; add to vegetable mixture and toss to coat. Sprinkle with Parmesan cheese if desired. **Yield:** 4 servings.

Ham and Vegetable Linguine

(Pictured above)

Kerry Kerr McAvoy, Rockford, Michigan

The delicate cream sauce blends well with the colorful and hearty mix of vegetables.

1 package (8 ounces) linguine
1/2 pound fresh asparagus, cut into 1-inch pieces
1/2 pound fresh mushrooms, sliced
1 medium carrot, thinly sliced
1 medium zucchini, diced
2 cups julienned fully cooked ham
1/4 cup butter
1 cup heavy whipping cream
1/2 cup frozen peas
3 green onions, sliced
1/4 cup grated Parmesan cheese
1 teaspoon dried basil
3/4 teaspoon salt
Dash *each* pepper and ground nutmeg
Additional Parmesan cheese, optional

Cook linguine according to package directions. Meanwhile, in a large skillet, saute asparagus, mushrooms, carrot, zucchini and ham in butter

Fettuccine Alfredo

Nikki Best, Littleton, Colorado

The original version of this recipe came from my sister, but I've added and subtracted ingredients to suit my family's tastes. It's something I can whip up at the last minute to feed guests who arrive unexpectedly. They always love it!

1 package (9 ounces) refrigerated fettuccine
1 cup broccoli florets
1 cup cauliflowerets
1/2 small onion, chopped
2 tablespoons olive oil
8 to 10 medium mushrooms, sliced
1 garlic clove, minced
2 cups diced fully cooked ham *or* chicken
1 jar (17 ounces) Alfredo sauce
Pepper to taste
Shredded Parmesan cheese

Make It 'Al Dente'

To test pasta for doneness, remove a single piece of pasta from the boiling water with a fork; rinse under cold water and taste. Pasta should be cooked until "al dente," tender but still firm to the bite. When you're testing for doneness, remember that residual heat continues to cook the pasta for a few seconds after it's removed from the water.

Test pasta often while cooking to avoid overcooking, which can result in a soft or mushy texture. If pasta will be used in a recipe that requires further cooking, such as a casserole, undercook it by one-third the recommended time. The pasta will continue to cook and absorb liquid in the final dish.

Cook fettuccine according to package directions. Meanwhile, in a large skillet, saute broccoli, cauliflower and onion in oil until tender. Add mushrooms and garlic; cook and stir for 3 minutes or until vegetables are crisp-tender.

Stir in the ham, Alfredo sauce and pepper. Cook until heated through. Drain fettuccine; toss with sauce. Sprinkle with Parmesan cheese. **Yield:** 4 servings.

Beef and Pepper Linguine

Marilyn Chigas, Peabody, Massachusetts

This recipe didn't sound so tasty when I first saw it, so I didn't make it for years. One day I decided to give it a try, and I'm glad I did!

- **1 pound ground beef**
- **1 large onion, chopped**
- **2 medium green peppers, cubed**
- **1 package (16 ounces) linguine, cooked and drained**
- **4 to 6 tablespoons soy sauce**
- **Dash garlic powder, optional**

In a large skillet, cook beef, onion and green peppers over medium heat until meat is no longer pink; drain. Remove from the heat. Add linguine and soy sauce; mix well. Sprinkle with garlic powder if desired. **Yield:** 6 servings.

Fabulous Fettuccine

(Pictured at right)

Mary Kay Morris, Cokato, Minnesota

My mother-in-law is from Italy, so my husband, Bob, grew up eating pasta dishes. I've been preparing this fresh-tasting version for many years. Bob requests it often, and even his mom thinks it's very good.

- **1/2 pound sliced bacon, diced**
- **3 tablespoons olive oil**
- **2 large onions, chopped**
- **3 pounds fresh tomatoes, peeled, seeded and chopped *or* 2 cans (14-1/2 ounces *each*) diced tomatoes, undrained**
- **3 garlic cloves, minced**
- **2 tablespoons minced fresh tarragon *or* 2 teaspoons dried tarragon**
- **1/2 teaspoon salt**
- **1/4 teaspoon pepper**
- **Pinch to 1/8 teaspoon cayenne pepper**
- **1 pound fettuccine**
- **1/4 cup minced fresh parsley**
- **Shredded Parmesan cheese**

In a skillet, cook bacon until crisp. Remove to paper towels. Drain, reserving 1 tablespoon drippings. Add oil and onions to drippings; saute until tender, about 5 minutes. Add tomatoes and garlic; simmer, uncovered, for 5 minutes. Stir in tarragon, salt, pepper and cayenne; cover and simmer for 20 minutes, stirring occasionally.

Meanwhile, cook fettuccine according to package directions. Add parsley to the tomato mixture; simmer 5 minutes longer. Stir in bacon. Drain fettuccine; top with tomato mixture. Sprinkle with Parmesan cheese. **Yield:** 4-6 servings.

Herbed Chicken Fettuccine

(Pictured below)

Kathy Kirkland, Denham Springs, Louisiana

Savory seasonings add zip to these moist chicken strips tossed with pasta. Every time I fix this dish, the kids ask for more.

- **1 to 2 teaspoons salt-free seasoning blend**
- **1 teaspoon poultry seasoning**
- **1 pound boneless skinless chicken breasts, cut into 1-inch strips**
- **2 tablespoons olive oil**
- **4 tablespoons butter, *divided***
- **2/3 cup water**
- **2 tablespoons teriyaki sauce**
- **2 tablespoons onion soup mix**
- **1 envelope savory herb and garlic soup mix, *divided***
- **8 ounces uncooked fettuccine**
- **2 tablespoons grated Parmesan cheese**
- **1 tablespoon Worcestershire sauce**

Combine seasoning blend and poultry seasoning; sprinkle over chicken. In a skillet, saute chicken in oil and 2 tablespoons butter for 5 minutes or until juices run clear. Add the water, teriyaki sauce, onion soup mix and 2 tablespoons herb and garlic soup mix. Bring to a boil. Reduce heat; cover and simmer for 15 minutes.

Meanwhile, cook the fettuccine according to package directions. Drain; add to the chicken mixture. Add cheese, Worcestershire sauce, remaining butter, and remaining herb and garlic soup mix; toss to coat. **Yield:** 4 servings.

Mushroom Ham Fettuccine

Renee Reyes, Owensboro, Kentucky

This entree tastes rich but it won't break the bank. It's one of our favorite pasta dishes and elegant enough for company.

- **1/2 pound thinly sliced fully cooked ham, cut into strips**
- **1 cup sliced fresh mushrooms**
- **2 garlic cloves, minced**
- **3 tablespoons plus 1/2 cup butter, *divided***
- **1 package (12 ounces) fettuccine**
- **1 cup grated Parmesan cheese**
- **1 cup (8 ounces) sour cream**
- **1/4 teaspoon pepper**

In a skillet, saute the ham, mushrooms and garlic in 3 tablespoons butter. Meanwhile, cook fettuccine according to package directions; drain.

Melt the remaining butter in a large saucepan. Stir in the fettuccine, Parmesan cheese, sour cream and pepper. Add the ham mixture; toss to coat. **Yield:** 8 servings.

Four-Seafood Fettuccine

Jeri Dobrowski, Beach, North Dakota

Here's an easy entree that tastes like you spent hours in the kitchen.

- **12 ounces fettuccine**
- **2 garlic cloves, minced**
- **3 tablespoons butter**

3 tablespoons all-purpose flour
1 cup milk
1 can (12 ounces) evaporated milk
1 cup cooked *or* canned crabmeat, drained, flaked and cartilage removed
1 cup cooked *or* canned lobster, drained and chopped
1 can (6-1/2 ounces) chopped clams, drained
1 can (4-1/2 ounces) tiny shrimp, drained
1/2 cup shredded Parmesan cheese
1 tablespoon minced fresh parsley
1/4 teaspoon pepper

Cook fettuccine according to package directions. Meanwhile, in a large saucepan, saute garlic in butter. Stir in flour until blended. Gradually add milk and evaporated milk.

Bring to a boil; cook and stir for 2 minutes or thickened. Add the crab, lobster, clams, shrimp, Parmesan cheese, parsley and pepper; heat through. Drain fettuccine; top with seafood mixture. **Yield:** 6 servings.

Linguine Alfredo

Loretta Ruda, Kennesaw, Georgia

Use up leftover noodles by tossing them with this wonderful creamy garlic sauce. This is my version of several recipes I've tried through the years. It is so simple to make. You can even top this dish with broiled shrimp or scallops.

1/4 teaspoon minced garlic
2 tablespoons butter
1/2 cup half-and-half cream
1-1/2 teaspoons minced fresh parsley, *divided*
1 teaspoon cornstarch
1 teaspoon cold water
1/4 cup grated Parmesan cheese
2 cups cooked linguine
Salt and pepper to taste

In a large saucepan, saute garlic in butter. Stir in the cream and 1 teaspoon parsley. Combine cornstarch and water until smooth; stir into cream mixture. Bring to a boil; cook and stir for 2 minutes or until thickened.

Remove from the heat; stir in the Parmesan cheese until melted. Toss with linguine; sprinkle with salt, pepper and remaining parsley. **Yield:** 2 servings.

Garlic Salmon Linguine

(Pictured above)

Theresa Hagan, Glendale, Arizona

This garlic-seasoned main dish calls for handy pantry ingredients, including pasta and canned salmon. I serve it with asparagus, rolls and fruit.

1 package (16 ounces) linguine
3 garlic cloves, minced
1/3 cup olive oil
1 can (14-3/4 ounces) salmon, drained, bones and skin removed
3/4 cup chicken broth
1/4 cup minced fresh parsley
1/2 teaspoon salt
1/8 teaspoon cayenne pepper

Cook the linguine according to package directions. Meanwhile, in a large skillet, saute garlic in oil. Stir in the salmon, broth, parsley, salt and cayenne. Cook until heated through. Drain linguine; add to the salmon mixture and toss to coat. **Yield:** 6 servings.

Turkey Linguine

(Pictured above)

Audrey Thibodeau, Mesa, Arizona

Here's a pleasing pasta and turkey combination I concocted to use when I'm in a hurry. It's a quick, delicious and complete meal that I frequently serve to guests. You may want to keep it a secret that you prepared this attractive, colorful skillet dish in just half an hour!

1 pound boneless turkey breast, cut into 1/2-inch strips
1 tablespoon olive oil
1/2 cup chopped onion
2 garlic cloves, minced
1 cup broccoli florets
1 cup thinly sliced carrots
1 tablespoon minced fresh basil *or* 1 teaspoon dried basil
1 teaspoon minced fresh tarragon *or* 1/4 teaspoon dried tarragon
1 teaspoon minced fresh thyme *or* 1/4 teaspoon dried thyme
1/8 teaspoon pepper
2 tablespoons cornstarch
1-1/2 cups chicken broth
8 ounces linguine, cooked
1/2 cup grated Parmesan cheese

In a large skillet or wok, stir-fry the turkey in oil for 2 minutes. Add the onion and garlic; cook and stir for 1 minute. Add the broccoli, carrots, basil, tarragon, thyme and pepper; stir-fry for 3-4 minutes or until the vegetables are crisp-tender.

Combine cornstarch and broth until smooth; add to the turkey mixture. Cook and stir until the mixture comes to a boil; cook 2 minutes longer. Serve over linguine; sprinkle with Parmesan cheese. **Yield:** 4 servings.

Pepper Steak Fettuccine

(Pictured on page 74)

Crystal West, New Straitsville, Ohio

My husband is a pasta lover, so I created this tangy dish myself, just for him. Strips of round steak, green pepper and onion make it a hearty and filling meal in one.

1-1/4 pounds boneless beef round steak (1/2 inch thick), cut into thin strips
1 medium green pepper, julienned
1 medium onion, julienned
2 tablespoons butter
2 cans (15 ounces *each*) tomato sauce
1 can (4 ounces) mushroom stems and pieces, drained
1-1/2 teaspoons salt
1 teaspoon dried basil
1/4 teaspoon pepper
1 package (16 ounces) fettuccine
1/3 cup shredded Parmesan cheese

In a large skillet, saute the steak, green pepper and onion in butter until meat is no longer pink. Stir in tomato sauce, mushrooms, salt, basil and pepper. Bring to a boil. Reduce heat; cover and simmer for 20-25 minutes or until meat is tender.

Cook fettuccine according to package directions; drain. Top with steak mixture; sprinkle with Parmesan cheese. **Yield:** 6 servings.

Vegetarian Linguine

(Pictured below right and on front cover)

Jane Bone, Cape Coral, Florida

Looking for a tasty alternative to meat-and-potatoes meals? Try this colorful pasta dish, which is the brainchild of my oldest son. It's a stick-to-the-ribs supper that takes advantage of fresh mushrooms, zucchini and other vegetables as well as basil and provolone cheese.

6 ounces uncooked linguine
2 medium zucchini, thinly sliced
1/2 pound fresh mushrooms, sliced
2 green onions, chopped
1 garlic clove, minced
2 tablespoons butter
1 tablespoon olive oil
1 large tomato, chopped
2 teaspoons minced fresh basil
1/2 teaspoon salt
1/4 teaspoon pepper
4 ounces provolone cheese, shredded
3 tablespoons shredded Parmesan cheese

Cook linguine according to package directions. Meanwhile, in a large skillet, saute the zucchini, mushrooms, onions and garlic in butter and oil for 3-5 minutes.

Add the tomato, basil, salt and pepper; cover and simmer for 3 minutes. Drain linguine; add to vegetable mixture. Sprinkle with cheeses and toss to coat. **Yield:** 6 servings.

Cajun Fettuccine

Jackie Turnage, New Iberia, Louisiana

It's nice to serve this zesty creamy casserole when you want a change from pasta dishes with a tomato sauce. The Cajun flavor really reflects this region of the country.

1-1/2 pounds ground beef
1 cup chopped green onions
1 medium onion, chopped
1 medium green pepper, chopped
1 celery rib, chopped
1 garlic clove, minced
1/4 cup butter
1 tablespoon all-purpose flour
8 ounces plain *or* Mexican-flavored process American cheese, cubed, *divided*
1 can (10 ounces) diced tomatoes and green chilies, undrained
1 can (5 ounces) evaporated milk
3/4 teaspoon Cajun *or* Creole seasoning
8 ounces fettuccine, cooked and drained
Grated Parmesan cheese

In a large skillet, cook beef over medium heat until no longer pink; drain and set aside. In the same skillet, saute the onions, green pepper, celery and garlic in butter until crisp-tender. Stir in flour until blended.

Return beef to the pan. Cook, uncovered, over medium heat for 15 minutes, stirring occasionally. Add 1 cup American cheese, tomatoes, milk and Cajun seasoning. Simmer, uncovered, for 15 minutes, stirring occasionally. Add fettuccine; mix well.

Transfer to a greased shallow 3-qt. baking dish. Top with remaining American cheese. Sprinkle with Parmesan cheese. Bake, uncovered, at 350° for 15 minutes or until heated through. **Yield:** 6-8 servings.

Walnut Ham Linguine

(Pictured below)

Mike Pickerel, Columbia, Missouri

This easy skillet dish is a pleasing combination of colors, textures and flavors. Garlic seasons this dish wonderfully. It's filling served alone, but it's also nice with a side mixed greens salad.

- **1 package (16 ounces) linguine *or* thin spaghetti**
- **2 to 4 garlic cloves, minced**
- **1/4 cup olive oil**
- **1/2 cup coarsely chopped walnuts**
- **1/2 pound fully cooked ham slices, cut into 1/2-inch strips**
- **1/3 cup grated Parmesan cheese**
- **1/4 cup minced fresh parsley**

Cook pasta according to package directions. Meanwhile, in a large skillet, saute garlic in oil for 1 minute. Add walnuts; saute for 2 minutes. Stir in ham; cook until heated through, about 2 minutes.

Drain pasta and toss with the ham mixture. Sprinkle with Parmesan cheese and parsley. **Yield:** 4-6 servings.

Creamy Shrimp Linguine

Jackie Hannahs, Cadillac, Michigan

My husband loves shrimp, so I'm always looking for different ways to fix it. This easy recipe tastes so good because of the fresh garlic.

- **8 ounces uncooked linguine**
- **3/4 cup chopped onion**
- **2 garlic cloves, minced**
- **1-1/2 teaspoons dried oregano**
- **3 tablespoons butter**
- **3/4 cup heavy whipping cream**
- **3/4 cup shredded Swiss cheese**
- **3/4 cup shredded Parmesan cheese**
- **1 pound cooked small shrimp, peeled and deveined**

Cook linguine according to package directions. Meanwhile, in a saucepan, saute the onion, garlic and oregano in butter until onion is crisp-tender. Gradually add the cream and cheeses; cook and stir over low heat until cheese is melted. Add the shrimp; heat through. Drain linguine; top with shrimp mixture. **Yield:** 4 servings.

Salmon Fettuccine

Lisa Royston, Wasilla, Alaska

This recipe is a great use for the salmon my husband often brings home.

- **8 ounces uncooked fettuccine**
- **1-1/2 cups sliced fresh mushrooms**
- **1 small zucchini, sliced**
- **2 tablespoons chopped onion**
- **2 tablespoons butter**
- **1 tablespoon all-purpose flour**
- **3/4 cup milk**
- **3/4 cup canned *or* cooked salmon chunks**
- **1/2 cup frozen peas, thawed**
- **1/2 cup diced fresh tomato**
- **1 tablespoon minced parsley**
- **1/4 teaspoon salt**
- **1/8 to 1/4 teaspoon pepper**
- **1/8 teaspoon dried basil**
- **1/8 teaspoon dried oregano**

Cook fettuccine according to package directions. Meanwhile, in a large skillet, saute the mushrooms, zucchini and onion in butter until crisp-tender. Stir in flour until blended. Gradually add milk.

Bring to a boil; cook and stir for 1 minute or until thickened. Add the salmon, peas, tomato, parsley and seasonings; heat through. Drain fettuccine; top with salmon mixture. **Yield:** 4 servings.

Two-Cheese Linguine

Taste of Home Test Kitchen

An easy cheese sauce turns ordinary pasta into a special side dish that's the perfect accompaniment to steak.

- **1 package (7 ounces) linguine**
- **2 tablespoons butter**
- **3 tablespoons all-purpose flour**
- **1/4 teaspoon salt**
- **1/8 teaspoon pepper**
- **1-1/2 cups milk**
- **3/4 cup (6 ounces) shredded mozzarella cheese**
- **1/4 cup shredded Parmesan cheese**
- **2 tablespoons lemon juice**

Cook linguine according to package directions. Meanwhile, in a skillet over low heat, melt butter. Stir in flour, salt and pepper until smooth. Gradually stir in milk. Bring to a boil; boil and stir for 2 minutes or until thickened. Remove from the heat. Combine cheeses; toss with lemon juice. Add to the sauce; stir until cheese begins to melt. Drain linguine; add the cheese sauce and toss to coat. **Yield:** 2 servings.

Bacon Chicken Alfredo

(Pictured above right)

Dana Simmons, Lancaster, Ohio

I had a rich pasta dish similar to this at a restaurant. It was so unique that I tried to duplicate it at home a few days later. This is remarkably close, but not as fussy because it uses ready-made ingredients rather than being made from scratch.

- **1 package (16 ounces) fettuccine**
- **1 pound sliced bacon, diced**
- **1-1/4 pounds boneless skinless chicken breasts, cubed**
- **1/4 teaspoon salt**
- **1/4 teaspoon pepper**
- **1 jar (16 ounces) prepared Alfredo sauce**
- **1 package (10 ounces) frozen chopped spinach, thawed and squeezed dry**
- **1/2 teaspoon Italian seasoning**
- **1/4 cup grated Parmesan cheese**

Cook fettuccine according to package directions. Meanwhile, in a large skillet, cook bacon over medium heat until crisp. Using a slotted spoon, remove to paper towels; drain, reserving 3 tablespoons drippings.

Sprinkle the chicken with salt and pepper. Cook chicken in the drippings over medium-high heat until the juices run clear.

Drain fettuccine; stir into skillet. Add the Alfredo sauce, spinach, Italian seasoning and bacon. Cook and stir until heated through. Sprinkle with Parmesan cheese. **Yield:** 6-8 servings.

Straw and Hay

(Pictured above)

Ardinelle Dover, Yreka, California

Years after I clipped this recipe from a local newspaper, it's still one of my husband's and my favorites. Sometimes I substitute shrimp or scallops for the ham.

1 cup milk
1/2 cup small-curd cottage cheese
1 tablespoon cornstarch
1/4 teaspoon salt
1/4 teaspoon pepper
1/8 teaspoon ground nutmeg
1/2 cup shredded Parmesan cheese, *divided*
4 ounces uncooked fettuccine
4 ounces uncooked spinach fettuccine
1/2 cup cubed fully cooked ham (4 ounces)
1 garlic clove, minced
1/2 cup frozen peas, thawed

In a blender or food processor, combine the milk, cottage cheese and cornstarch; cover and process until smooth. Transfer to a saucepan; add salt, pepper and nutmeg. Cook and stir over medium heat until mixture comes to a boil. Remove from the heat; stir in 1/4 cup Parmesan cheese until melted.

Cook fettuccine according to package directions. Meanwhile, in a large nonstick skillet coated with nonstick cooking spray, heat ham and garlic for 2 minutes. Add peas; heat through. Remove from the heat; stir in cheese sauce. Drain fettuccine; toss with sauce. Sprinkle with remaining Parmesan. **Yield:** 6 servings.

Linguine with Garlic Clam Sauce

Perlene Hoekema, Lynden, Washington

Keep the ingredients for this 30-minute entree on hand for supper in a snap!

1 package (8 ounces) linguine
2 to 3 garlic cloves, minced
5 tablespoons butter
1/4 cup olive oil
1 tablespoon all-purpose flour
2 cans (6-1/2 ounces *each*) minced clams
1 cup (4 ounces) shredded Monterey Jack cheese
1/4 cup minced fresh parsley

Cook linguine according to package directions. Meanwhile, in a skillet, saute garlic in butter and oil until golden. Stir in flour until blended. Drain clams, reserving juice; set clams aside. Gradually add juice to the skillet. Bring to a boil; cook and stir for 2 minutes or until thickened. Reduce heat; stir in clams, cheese and parsley. Cook until cheese is melted and sauce has thickened. Drain linguine; top with clam sauce. **Yield:** 4 servings.

Cajun Chicken Pasta

Tracy Price, South Hadley, Massachusetts

The Cajun Chicken Pasta at the Monroe Street Grille in Tallahassee, Florida is so good that I was thrilled to get the recipe. Cream pairs well with the Cajun and lemon-pepper seasoning.

2 boneless skinless chicken breast halves, cut into thin strips
2 teaspoons Cajun seasoning
2 tablespoons butter
8 slices *each* green and sweet red pepper
4 large fresh mushrooms, sliced

1 green onion, sliced
1 to 2 cups heavy whipping cream
1/4 teaspoon dried basil
1/4 teaspoon lemon-pepper seasoning
1/4 teaspoon salt
1/8 teaspoon garlic powder
1/8 teaspoon pepper
4 ounces linguine, cooked and drained
Grated Parmesan cheese, optional

Place chicken and Cajun seasoning in a bowl or resealable plastic bag; toss or shake to coat. In a large skillet over medium heat, saute chicken in butter until almost tender, about 5-7 minutes. Add peppers, mushrooms and onion; cook and stir for 2-3 minutes. Reduce heat. Add cream and seasonings; heat through. Add linguine and toss; heat through. Sprinkle with Parmesan cheese if desired. **Yield:** 2 servings.

Pesto Red Pepper Pasta

Taste of Home Test Kitchen

Our staff created this from-scratch pesto that comes together in minutes. Roasted sweet red peppers steal the show in the savory dish.

1 package (1 pound) linguine
2 cups loosely packed fresh basil leaves
1/2 cup whole blanched almonds
4 garlic cloves, peeled
1 cup olive oil
1/2 cup grated Parmesan cheese
1/4 cup grated Romano cheese
1/4 teaspoon salt
Dash pepper
1 cup chopped roasted sweet red peppers

Cook linguine according to package directions. Meanwhile, for pesto, combine the basil, almonds and garlic in a blender or food processor; cover and process for 1 minute or until finely chopped. While processing, gradually add oil in a steady stream.

Add the cheeses, salt and pepper; pulse until combined. Drain linguine; toss with pesto and roasted peppers. **Yield:** 6-8 servings.

Chicken Scampi

(Pictured below)

Janet Lebar, Littleton, Colorado

This recipe is so delectable that I'm often asked to double it when family members visit over the holidays.

4 ounces uncooked linguine
2 green onions, thinly sliced
2 garlic cloves, minced
3 tablespoons butter
2 tablespoons olive oil
2 boneless skinless chicken breast halves
1/2 teaspoon salt
1/4 teaspoon coarsely ground pepper
1/2 cup chopped seeded tomato
2 tablespoons lemon juice
1 tablespoon minced fresh parsley
Grated Parmesan cheese

Cook linguine according to package directions. Meanwhile, in a skillet, saute the onions and garlic in butter and oil until garlic is tender. Sprinkle chicken with salt and pepper; add to skillet. Cook for 3 minutes on each side or until lightly browned.

Reduce heat; cover and cook 4 minutes longer or until juices run clear. Remove chicken and keep warm. Stir the tomato, lemon juice and parsley into skillet; heat through. Drain linguine; toss with tomato mixture. Top with chicken and sprinkle with Parmesan cheese. **Yield:** 2 servings.

Casserol

Veggie Noodle Ham Casserole (p. 93)

Turkey Tetrazzini

(Pictured above)

Susan Payne, Corner Brook, Newfoundland

I make this recipe with leftover turkey, and it's a whole new meal! We look forward to having it after Christmas, Thanksgiving and other times I have leftover turkey.

1 package (7 ounces) thin spaghetti, broken in half
2 cups cubed cooked turkey
1 cup sliced fresh mushrooms
1 small onion, chopped
3 tablespoons butter
1 can (10-3/4 ounces) condensed cream of mushroom soup, undiluted
1 cup milk
1/2 teaspoon poultry seasoning
1/8 teaspoon ground mustard
1 cup (4 ounces) shredded cheddar cheese
1 cup (4 ounces) shredded mozzarella cheese
1 tablespoon shredded Parmesan cheese
Minced fresh parsley

Cook spaghetti according to package directions. Drain and place in a greased 11-in. x 7-in. x 2-in. baking dish. Top with turkey; set aside.

In a skillet, saute the mushrooms and onion in butter until tender. Whisk in the soup, milk, poultry seasoning and mustard until blended. Stir in the cheddar cheese; cook and stir over medium heat until cheese is melted. Pour over turkey.

Sprinkle with mozzarella and Parmesan cheeses (dish will be full). Bake, uncovered, at 350° for 25-30 minutes or until heated through and cheese is melted. Sprinkle with parsley. **Yield:** 4-6 servings.

Angel Hair Shrimp Bake

Susan Davidson, Elm Grove, Wisconsin

Shrimp and pasta blend beautifully with the herbs, salsa and three kinds of cheese in this hearty layered casserole. The shrimp make this dish special enough for guests, but your family is sure to enjoy it, too.

1 package (9 ounces) refrigerated angel hair pasta
1-1/2 pounds uncooked medium shrimp, peeled and deveined
3/4 cup crumbled feta cheese
1/2 cup shredded Swiss cheese
1 jar (16 ounces) chunky salsa
1/2 cup shredded Monterey Jack cheese
3/4 cup minced fresh parsley
1 teaspoon dried basil
1 teaspoon dried oregano
2 eggs
1 cup half-and-half cream
1 cup (8 ounces) plain yogurt

In a greased 13-in. x 9-in. x 2-in. baking dish, layer half of the pasta, shrimp, feta cheese, Swiss cheese and salsa. Repeat layers. Sprinkle with Monterey Jack cheese, parsley, basil and oregano.

In a small bowl, whisk eggs, cream and yogurt; pour over casserole. Bake, uncovered, at 350° for 25-30 minutes or until shrimp turn pink and pasta is tender. Let stand for 5 minutes before serving. **Yield:** 12 servings.

Polish Reuben Casserole

Imogene Peterson, Ontario, Oregon

People are always asking me for this recipe. It's easy to assemble and great to take to potlucks, which we have a lot of in our community.

1 package (8 ounces) egg noodles
2 cans (14 ounces *each*) Bavarian sauerkraut, drained
2 cans (10-3/4 ounces *each*) condensed cream of mushroom soup, undiluted
1-1/3 cups milk
1 medium onion, chopped
1 tablespoon prepared mustard
1-1/2 pounds Polish sausage *or* kielbasa, halved and cut into 1/2-inch slices
2 cups (8 ounces) shredded Swiss cheese
1/2 cup soft rye bread crumbs
2 tablespoons butter, melted

Cook noodles according to package directions; drain. Spread sauerkraut in a greased shallow 4-qt. baking dish. Top with noodles. In a bowl, combine the soup, milk, onion and mustard; pour over the noodles. Top with sausage; sprinkle with cheese.

Combine bread crumbs and butter; sprinkle over the top. Cover and bake at 350° for 30-35 minutes or until heated through. **Yield:** 12-14 servings.

Company Casserole

(Pictured at right)

Marcia McCutchan, Hamilton, Ohio

I concocted this recipe one day while trying to straighten up my canned goods cupboard. Friends and relatives have told me how much they like it. Many have asked for the recipe.

8 ounces process cheese (Velveeta), cubed
1/4 cup milk
2 cans (14-1/2 ounces *each*) diced tomatoes, undrained
3/4 cup mayonnaise
1 tablespoon Worcestershire sauce
4 cups cubed fully cooked ham
4 cups cooked elbow macaroni
1 package (10 ounces) frozen chopped broccoli, thawed and drained
1 package (10 ounces) frozen peas, thawed
1 small green pepper, chopped
1 small onion, chopped
1/2 cup crushed stuffing mix
1 can (2.8 ounces) french-fried onions, chopped, optional
1 cup soft bread crumbs
1/4 cup butter, melted

In a large saucepan, cook and stir cheese and milk over low heat until cheese is melted. Stir in tomatoes until blended. Remove from the heat; stir in the mayonnaise and Worcestershire sauce until blended. Stir in the ham, macaroni, broccoli, peas, green pepper, onion, stuffing mix and onions if desired.

Transfer to two greased 2-1/2-qt. baking dishes. Toss bread crumbs and butter; sprinkle over the top. Bake, uncovered, at 350° for 35-40 minutes or until bubbly. **Yield:** 2 casseroles (8-10 servings each).

Editor's Note: Reduced-fat or fat-free mayonnaise may not be substituted for regular mayonnaise in this recipe.

Baked Ziti

(Pictured below)

Elaine Anderson, Aliquippa, Pennsylvania

I enjoy making this dish for family and friends. It's easy to prepare, and I like to get creative with the sauce. For example, sometimes I might add my home-canned tomatoes, mushrooms or other vegetables. With garlic bread and a green salad, you have an easy Italian meal. Any kind of cheesecake makes a wonderful dessert.

- **12 ounces uncooked ziti *or* small tube pasta**
- **2 pounds ground beef**
- **1 jar (28 ounces) spaghetti sauce**
- **2 eggs**
- **1 carton (15 ounces) ricotta cheese**
- **2-1/2 cups (10 ounces) shredded mozzarella cheese, *divided***
- **1/2 cup grated Parmesan cheese**

Cook pasta according to package directions. Meanwhile, in a skillet, cook beef over medium heat until no longer pink; drain. Stir in spaghetti sauce. In a bowl, combine the eggs, ricotta cheese, 1-1/2 cups mozzarella cheese and Parmesan cheese.

Drain pasta; add to cheese mixture and toss to coat. Spoon a third of the meat sauce into a greased 13-in. x 9-in. x 2-in. baking dish; top with half of the pasta mixture. Repeat layers. Top with remaining meat sauce.

Cover and bake at 350° for 40 minutes. Uncover; sprinkle with remaining mozzarella cheese. Bake 5-10 minutes longer or until the cheese is melted. Let stand for 15 minutes before serving. **Yield:** 6-8 servings.

Cheesy Mac 'n' Dogs

Sue Gonzales, Fortson, Georgia

I've made this casserole for over 25 years now and my family never gets tired of it. I like to assemble it the night before, then pop it in the oven after a busy day at work. A tossed salad completes the meal nicely.

- **1 package (8 ounces) elbow macaroni**
- **1 small onion, finely chopped**
- **1/4 cup butter**
- **1/4 cup all-purpose flour**
- **1 teaspoon salt**
- **1/2 teaspoon ground mustard**
- **2-1/2 cups milk**
- **3/4 teaspoon Worcestershire sauce**
- **12 ounces process cheese (Velveeta), cubed**
- **7 cooked hot dogs, diced**
- **1/4 cup dry bread crumbs**

Cook macaroni according to package directions. Meanwhile, in a large skillet, saute onion in butter until tender. Stir in the flour, salt and mustard. Gradually add milk. Bring to a boil; cook and stir for 2 minutes or until thickened. Stir in the Worcestershire sauce and cheese until cheese is melted.

Drain macaroni; stir into the cheese sauce. Add the hot dogs. Transfer to a greased 2-1/2-qt. baking dish. Sprinkle with bread crumbs. Bake, uncovered, at 350° for 20-25 minutes or until bubbly. **Yield:** 6-8 servings.

Oriental Beef Noodle Toss

Sue Livangood, Waukesha, Wisconsin

I received this recipe from a friend who is a nurse. We always share new recipes, especially for easy meals like this, because our schedules keep us both quite busy.

1 pound ground beef
2 packages (3 ounces *each*) Oriental-flavored ramen noodles
1 package (16 ounces) frozen Oriental vegetable blend
2 cups water
4 to 5 tablespoons soy sauce
1/4 teaspoon ground ginger
3 tablespoons thinly sliced green onions

In a large skillet, cook beef over medium heat until no longer pink; drain. Stir in contents of one noodle seasoning packet; set aside and keep warm.

Break the noodles; place in a large saucepan. Add the contents of second seasoning packet, vegetables, water, soy sauce and ginger. Bring to a boil. Reduce heat; cover and simmer for 6-10 minutes or until vegetables and noodles are tender. Stir in the beef and onions. **Yield:** 4-6 servings.

Spinach Beef Macaroni Bake

(Pictured above right)

Lois Lauppe, Lahoma, Oklahoma

This hearty casserole is great for a family reunion or church supper. I've also made half the recipe for family gatherings. It's become a special favorite of my grandson-in-law and great-grandson, who often ask me to serve it when they're visiting.

5-1/4 cups uncooked elbow macaroni
2-1/2 pounds ground beef
2 large onions, chopped
3 large carrots, shredded
3 celery ribs, chopped
2 cans (28 ounces *each*) Italian diced tomatoes, undrained
4 teaspoons salt
1 teaspoon garlic powder
1 teaspoon pepper
1/2 teaspoon dried oregano
2 packages (10 ounces *each*) frozen chopped spinach, thawed and squeezed dry
1 cup grated Parmesan cheese

Cook macaroni according to package directions. Meanwhile, in a Dutch oven or large kettle, cook the beef, onions, carrots and celery over medium heat until meat is no longer pink; drain. Add the tomatoes, salt, garlic powder, pepper and oregano. Bring to a boil. Reduce heat; cover and simmer for 30 minutes or until vegetables are tender.

Drain macaroni; add macaroni and spinach to beef mixture. Pour into two greased 3-qt. baking dishes. Sprinkle with Parmesan cheese. Bake, uncovered, at 350° for 25-30 minutes or until heated through. **Yield:** 2 casseroles (12 servings each).

In a large saucepan, saute green pepper and onion in 2 tablespoons butter until tender. Stir in the flour and salt until blended. Gradually stir in milk. Bring to a boil; cook and stir for 2 minutes or until thickened. Stir in tomato and parsley.

Remove from the heat; stir in 1 cup of cheese until melted. Stir in pasta and crab. Transfer to a greased shallow 2-1/2-qt. baking dish. Cover and bake at 350° for 20 minutes.

Melt the remaining butter; toss with bread crumbs. Sprinkle over casserole. Top with remaining cheese. Bake, uncovered, for 5-10 minutes or until golden brown. **Yield:** 6-8 servings.

Padre Island Shells

(Pictured above)

Dona Grover, Rockwall, Texas

I'm asked to fix this dish over and over, so there's no doubt it's worth sharing. People rave about the pasta and seafood combo.

- **1/2 cup chopped green pepper**
- **2 tablespoons thinly sliced green onion**
- **4 tablespoons butter, *divided***
- **2 tablespoons all-purpose flour**
- **1/2 teaspoon salt**
- **2 cups milk**
- **1 large tomato, peeled and chopped**
- **2 tablespoons minced fresh parsley**
- **1-1/4 cups shredded pepper Jack *or* Monterey Jack cheese, *divided***
- **3-1/2 cups medium shell pasta, cooked and drained**
- **3 cans (6 ounces *each*) crabmeat, drained, flaked and cartilage removed *or* 1 pound imitation crabmeat, flaked**
- **1/2 cup dry bread crumbs**

Cashew Noodle Casserole

Marion Petersson, Wetaskiwin, Alberta

Chow mein noodles and cashews give this dish a delectable crunch. You can make the casserole and freeze it; stir in the chow mein noodles just before serving.

- **2 pounds ground beef**
- **2 large onions, chopped**
- **1 can (4 ounces) mushroom stems and pieces, drained**
- **1 can (10-3/4 ounces) condensed cream of chicken soup, undiluted**
- **1-1/4 cups milk**
- **1/4 cup soy sauce**
- **1 teaspoon Worcestershire sauce**
- **1/2 teaspoon pepper**
- **8 ounces fine egg noodles, cooked and drained**
- **2 cups (8 ounces) shredded cheddar cheese**
- **1 package (6 ounces) chow mein noodles**
- **1 cup whole cashews**

In a skillet, cook beef and onions over medium heat until meat is no longer pink; drain. Add the mushrooms; set aside. In a bowl, combine the soup, milk, soy sauce, Worcestershire sauce and pepper.

In a greased 13-in. x 9-in. x 2-in. baking dish, layer egg noodles, beef mixture and soup mixture. Sprinkle with cheese and chow mein noodles. Bake, uncovered, at 350° for 20 minutes or until heated through. Sprinkle with cashews. **Yield:** 8-10 servings.

Veggie Noodle Ham Casserole

(Pictured on page 86)

Judy Moody, Wheatley, Ontario

This saucy main dish is quite versatile. Without the ham, it can be a vegetarian entree or a hearty side dish.

- **1 package (12 ounces) wide egg noodles**
- **1 can (10-3/4 ounces) condensed cream of chicken soup, undiluted**
- **1 can (10-3/4 ounces) condensed cream of broccoli soup, undiluted**
- **1-1/2 cups milk**
- **2 cups frozen corn, thawed**
- **1-1/2 cups frozen California-blend vegetables, thawed**
- **1-1/2 cups cubed fully cooked ham**
- **2 tablespoons minced fresh parsley**
- **1/2 teaspoon pepper**
- **1/4 teaspoon salt**
- **1 cup (4 ounces) shredded cheddar cheese, *divided***

Cook noodles according to package directions; drain. In a bowl, combine soups and milk; stir in the noodles, corn, vegetables, ham, parsley, pepper, salt and 3/4 cup of cheese. Transfer to a greased 13-in. x 9-in. x 2-in. baking dish.

Cover and bake at 350° for 45 minutes. Uncover; sprinkle with remaining cheese. Bake 5-10 minutes longer or until bubbly and cheese is melted. **Yield:** 8-10 servings.

Mom's Mostaccioli

(Pictured at right)

Gayle Clark, Neptune Beach, Florida

This traditional pasta dish has been a standby in my kitchen since the 1960s. My daughter and son have even added it to their own recipe box collections.

- **1/2 pound ground beef**
- **1 medium onion, chopped**
- **1/2 cup chopped green pepper**
- **1 can (14-1/2 ounces) diced tomatoes, undrained**
- **1 can (6 ounces) tomato paste**
- **1/2 cup water**
- **1 bay leaf**
- **1/2 teaspoon salt**
- **1/4 teaspoon pepper**
- **8 ounces mostaccioli, cooked and drained**
- **8 ounces sliced process American cheese**

In a skillet, cook beef, onion and green pepper over medium heat until meat is no longer pink; drain. Add the tomatoes, tomato paste, water, bay leaf, salt and pepper. Cover and simmer for 10 minutes; discard bay leaf.

In a greased 11-in. x 7-in. x 2-in. baking dish, layer half of the mostaccioli, meat sauce and cheese; repeat layers. Bake, uncovered, at 350° for 30 minutes or until heated through. Let stand for 10 minutes before serving. **Yield:** 4-6 servings.

Italian Casserole

(Pictured below)

Rita Goshaw, South Milwaukee, Wisconsin

I come from a huge family, and it seems there is always a potluck occasion. Come late spring, graduation parties are the perfect place for me to bring this hearty, crowd-pleasing Italian main dish. It's easy to make and serve.

1-1/2 pounds bulk Italian sausage
1-1/2 pounds ground beef
1 cup chopped onion
1 cup chopped green pepper
2 cans (15 ounces *each*) tomato sauce
2 cans (6 ounces *each*) tomato paste
1/2 cup water
1 teaspoon dried basil
1 teaspoon dried oregano
1 teaspoon salt
1 teaspoon pepper
1/8 teaspoon garlic powder
2 cans (8-3/4 ounces *each*) whole kernel corn, drained
2 cans (2-1/4 ounces *each*) sliced ripe olives, drained
1 package (16 ounces) wide egg noodles, cooked and drained
8 ounces cheddar cheese, cut into strips

Keeping Pasta Hot

To keep cooked pasta hot for a few minutes before using, return cooked and drained pasta to the warm cooking pan. Stir in any additional ingredients.

Pasta cools quickly, so always heat the serving bowl or plates before you dish it up. Dishes can be heated in a 250° oven until warm, about 10 minutes. Or fill a serving bowl with very hot water, then pour it out and dry the bowl before serving.

In a Dutch oven over medium heat, cook sausage, beef, onion and green pepper until meat is no longer pink and vegetables are tender; drain. Add tomato sauce and paste, water and seasonings; bring to a boil. Reduce heat; cover and simmer for 15 minutes. Add corn and olives; cover and simmer for 5 minutes. Stir in noodles.

Pour into two greased 13-in. x 9-in. x 2-in. baking dishes. Top with cheese. Cover and bake at 350° for 25-30 minutes or until heated through. **Yield:** 16-20 servings.

Cheesy Tuna Mac

Stephanie Martin, Macomb, Michigan

What could be easier than dressing up a boxed macaroni and cheese mix with tuna and canned soup? This comforting casserole is a snap to fix, and my two boys gobble it up. You can vary the soup and veggies to suit your family's tastes.

1 package (7-1/4 ounces) macaroni and cheese mix
1/2 cup milk
1 tablespoon butter
1 can (10-3/4 ounces) condensed cream of broccoli soup, undiluted
1 can (6 ounces) tuna, drained and flaked
3/4 cup frozen peas
2 tablespoons finely chopped onion
1 tablespoon process cheese sauce

Cook the macaroni according to package directions; drain. Stir in the milk, butter and contents of cheese packet. Add the soup, tuna, peas, onion and cheese sauce. Spoon into a greased 1-1/2-qt. baking dish. Cover and bake at 350° for 20 minutes. Uncover; bake 5-10 minutes longer or until heated through. **Yield:** 4 servings.

Turkey Macaroni Bake

Cherry Williams, St. Albert, Alberta

A co-worker gave me this recipe when we were discussing quick-and-easy ways to use leftover turkey. The mild cheesy casserole is a hit with my family. And it doesn't get much easier than this...you don't even have to cook the elbow macaroni first!

- **2 cups cubed cooked turkey**
- **1-1/2 cups uncooked elbow macaroni**
- **2 cups (8 ounces) shredded cheddar cheese, *divided***
- **1 can (10-3/4 ounces) condensed cream of chicken soup, undiluted**
- **1 cup milk**
- **1 can (8 ounces) mushroom stems and pieces, drained**
- **1/4 teaspoon pepper**

In a large bowl, combine the turkey, macaroni, 1-1/2 cups cheese, soup, milk, mushrooms and pepper. Pour into a greased 2-qt. baking dish.

Cover and bake at 350° for 60-65 minutes or until macaroni is tender. Uncover; sprinkle with remaining cheese. Bake 5-10 minutes longer or until cheese is melted. **Yield:** 6 servings.

Cheesy Sausage Penne

(Pictured above right)

Dallas McCord, Reno, Nevada

This lasagna-like entree takes me back to my childhood. I got the recipe from a friend's mother, who fixed it for us often when we were kids. I made a few changes to it, but it's still quick and delicious.

- **1 pound bulk Italian sausage**
- **1 garlic clove, minced**
- **1 jar (26 ounces) spaghetti sauce**
- **1 package (1 pound) penne *or* medium tube pasta**
- **1 package (8 ounces) cream cheese, softened**
- **1 cup (8 ounces) sour cream**
- **4 green onions, sliced**
- **2 cups (8 ounces) shredded cheddar cheese**

In a large skillet, cook the sausage and garlic over medium heat until meat is no longer pink; drain. Stir in spaghetti sauce; bring to a boil. Reduce heat; cover and simmer for 20 minutes. Meanwhile, cook pasta according to package directions; drain. In a small mixing bowl, combine the cream cheese, sour cream and onions.

In a greased shallow 3-qt. baking dish, layer half of the pasta and sausage mixture. Dollop with half of the cream cheese mixture; sprinkle with half of the cheddar cheese. Repeat layers. Bake, uncovered, at 350° for 30-35 minutes or until bubbly. **Yield:** 12 servings.

Cook spaghetti according to package directions. Meanwhile, in a large skillet, cook beef and onion over medium heat until meat is no longer pink; drain. Stir in the taco seasoning, spaghetti sauce, mushrooms and olives. Drain spaghetti; stir into the beef mixture.

Transfer to a greased shallow 3-qt. baking dish; sprinkle with cheese. Bake, uncovered, at 350° for 25-30 minutes or until heated through. Serve with lettuce, tomatoes, sour cream and salsa. **Yield:** 8 servings.

Tex-Mex Spaghetti

(Pictured above)

Rose Turner Minnick, Christiansburg, Virginia

A close friend made this Mexican-Italian bake for me almost 20 years ago, and I've prepared it regularly ever since. It comes together in a snap because it relies largely on convenience items I keep on hand. We like it with a loaf of crusty bread.

12 ounces uncooked spaghetti
1-1/2 pounds ground beef
1 small onion, chopped
1 envelope taco seasoning
1 jar (26 ounces) spaghetti sauce
1 jar (4-1/2 ounces) sliced mushrooms, drained
1 can (2-1/4 ounces) sliced ripe olives, drained
2 cups (8 ounces) shredded cheddar cheese
Shredded lettuce, diced tomatoes, sour cream and salsa *or* picante sauce

Chicken Spaghetti Casserole

Bernice Janowski, Stevens Point, Wisconsin

I first made this meal-in-one when I had unexpected guests. It's popular when I'm in a hurry, because it takes minutes to assemble.

8 ounces uncooked spaghetti
1 carton (8 ounces) ricotta cheese
1 cup (4 ounces) shredded mozzarella cheese, *divided*
2 tablespoons grated Parmesan cheese
1/2 teaspoon Italian seasoning
1/2 teaspoon garlic powder
1 jar (26 ounces) meatless spaghetti sauce
1 can (14-1/2 ounces) Italian diced tomatoes, undrained
1 jar (4-1/2 ounces) sliced mushrooms, drained
4 breaded fully cooked chicken patties (10 to 14 ounces)

Cook spaghetti according to package directions. Meanwhile, in a bowl, combine the ricotta, 1/2 cup of mozzarella, Parmesan, Italian seasoning and garlic powder; set aside. In another bowl, combine the spaghetti sauce, tomatoes and mushrooms.

Drain spaghetti; add 2 cups spaghetti sauce mixture and toss to coat. Transfer to a greased 13-in. x 9-in. x 2-in. baking dish; top with cheese mixture. Arrange chicken patties over the top; drizzle with the remaining spaghetti sauce mixture. Sprinkle with the remaining mozzarella. Bake, uncovered, at 350° for 40-45 minutes or until bubbly. **Yield:** 4 servings.

Bow Tie Turkey Bake

Betty Aiken, Bradenton, Florida

Quick—start the water boiling! In just 30 minutes, you can take one of these delicious noodle dishes from the stovetop (or the microwave) to the table.

- **2-1/2 cups uncooked bow tie pasta**
- **8 ounces turkey Italian sausage links, casings removed**
- **1 jar (26 ounces) spaghetti sauce**
- **3/4 cup cottage cheese, drained**
- **1/4 cup grated Parmesan cheese**
- **1 package (10 ounces) frozen chopped spinach, thawed and squeezed dry**
- **1 tablespoon shredded Parmesan cheese**

Cook pasta according to package directions. Meanwhile, in a skillet, cook sausage over medium heat until no longer pink; drain. Drain the noodles. Spread 1/4 cup spaghetti sauce in a greased 2-qt. microwave-safe dish. Layer with half of the noodles, a third of the remaining sauce and half of the cottage cheese, sausage and grated Parmesan.

Top with spinach. Repeat the layers of noodles, sauce, cottage cheese and grated Parmesan. Top with the remaining sauce. Sprinkle with shredded Parmesan. Cover and microwave on high for 8 minutes or until heated through. **Yield:** 4-6 servings.

Editor's Note: This recipe was tested in an 850-watt microwave.

Four-Pasta Beef Bake

(Pictured at right)

Harriet Stichter, Milford, Indiana

This hearty casserole looks and tastes a lot like lasagna, but it's quicker to prepare since you don't have to layer it. It disappears fast when I share it at a gathering. Served with rolls and a salad, it makes an easy and satisfying supper.

- **8 cups uncooked pasta (four different shapes)**
- **2 pounds ground beef**
- **2 medium green peppers, chopped**
- **2 medium onions, chopped**
- **2 cups sliced fresh mushrooms**
- **4 jars (26 ounces *each*) meatless spaghetti sauce**
- **2 eggs, lightly beaten**
- **4 cups (16 ounces) shredded mozzarella cheese**

Cook pasta according to package directions. Meanwhile, in a large skillet, cook the beef, green peppers, onions and mushrooms over medium heat until meat is no longer pink; drain.

Drain pasta and place in a large bowl; stir in the beef mixture, two jars of spaghetti sauce and eggs. Transfer to two greased 13-in. x 9-in. x 2-in. baking dishes. Top with remaining sauce; sprinkle with cheese. Bake, uncovered, at 350° for 25-30 minutes or until heated through. **Yield:** 2 casseroles (8-10 servings each).

Skillet
Dishes

Hamburger Macaroni Skillet (p.103)

Zippy Zucchini Pasta

(Pictured above)

Kathleen Timberlake
Dearborn Heights, Michigan

A colorful combination of zucchini and zippy canned tomatoes is delicious over quick-cooking angel hair pasta. We like the extra zest from crushed red pepper flakes.

1 package (7 ounces) angel hair pasta *or* thin spaghetti
2 small zucchini, sliced 1/4 inch thick
2 garlic cloves, minced
3 tablespoons olive oil
1 can (16 ounces) Mexican diced tomatoes, undrained
1/4 cup minced fresh parsley
1 teaspoon dried oregano
1/8 to 1/2 teaspoon crushed red pepper flakes

Cook pasta according to package directions. Meanwhile, in a skillet, saute zucchini and garlic in oil until zucchini is crisp-tender. Add the tomatoes, parsley, oregano and red pepper flakes; heat through. Drain pasta; top with zucchini mixture. **Yield:** 3 servings.

Tortellini Alfredo

Chris Snyder, Boulder, Colorado

Refrigerated tortellini, ham, mushrooms and peas are mixed with a mild homemade Alfredo sauce in this fast fix. When we're having company, I prepare this dinner shortly before guests arrive, put it in a casserole dish and keep it warm in the oven.

2 packages (9 ounces *each*) refrigerated cheese tortellini
1/2 cup chopped onion
1/3 cup butter
1-1/2 cups frozen peas, thawed
1 cup thinly sliced fresh mushrooms
1 cup cubed fully cooked ham
1-3/4 cups heavy whipping cream
1/4 teaspoon coarsely ground pepper
3/4 cup grated Parmesan cheese
Shredded Parmesan cheese, optional

Cook tortellini according to package directions. Meanwhile, in a skillet, saute the onion in butter until tender. Add the peas, mushrooms and ham; cook until mushrooms are tender. Stir in cream and pepper; heat through. Stir in grated Parmesan cheese until melted.

Drain tortellini and place in a serving dish; add the sauce and toss to coat. Sprinkle with the shredded Parmesan cheese if desired. **Yield:** 4-6 servings.

Jiffy Ground Pork Skillet

Brigitte Schaller, Flemington, Missouri

Some people call it dinner hour, but many of us call it rush hour. Slow down the pace with this

Use a Skillet

Try making your pasta sauce in a 12- or 14-inch skillet. That way, you can turn the drained pasta right into the skillet and have plenty of room to toss it.

super-quick mouth-watering meal. The only thing you'll have left over is time to share with your family.

1-1/2 cups uncooked penne *or* medium tube pasta
1 pound ground pork
1/2 cup chopped onion
1 can (14-1/2 ounces) stewed tomatoes
1 can (8 ounces) tomato sauce
1 teaspoon Italian seasoning
1 medium zucchini, cut into 1/4-inch slices

Cook pasta according to package directions. Meanwhile, in a large skillet, cook pork and onion over medium heat until meat is no longer pink; drain. Add the tomatoes, tomato sauce and Italian seasoning. Bring to a boil. Reduce heat; cover and cook for 5 minutes.

Drain pasta and add to the skillet. Stir in zucchini. Cover and cook for 3-5 minutes or until zucchini is crisp-tender. **Yield:** 6 servings.

Deluxe Macaroni Dinner

Michele Odstrcilek, Lemont, Illinois

This recipe never results in leftovers. I dress up a boxed mac-and-cheese mix with ground beef, onion and broccoli.

1/2 pound ground beef
1 small onion, chopped
2 garlic cloves, minced
10 cups water
1 package (14 ounces) deluxe four-cheese macaroni and cheese dinner
2 cups chopped fresh broccoli

In a large skillet, cook the beef, onion and garlic until meat is no longer pink; drain. In a large saucepan, bring the water to a boil. Add macaroni; cook for 5 minutes. Add broccoli; cook 4-5 minutes longer or until macaroni and broccoli are tender.

Drain, reserving 1/4 cup cooking liquid. Place contents of cheese sauce mix in saucepan. Stir in macaroni mixture, beef mixture and reserved liquid; heat through. **Yield:** 4-6 servings.

Spanish Noodles 'n' Ground Beef

(Pictured below)

Kelli Jones, Perris, California

Bacon adds flavor to this comforting stovetop supper my mom frequently made when we were growing up. Now I prepare it for my family. It disappears quickly.

1 pound ground beef
1 small green pepper, chopped
1 small onion, chopped
3-1/4 cups uncooked medium egg noodles
1 can (14-1/2 ounces) diced tomatoes, undrained
1 cup water
1/4 cup chili sauce
1 teaspoon salt
1/8 teaspoon pepper
4 bacon strips, cooked and crumbled

In a large skillet over medium heat, cook the beef, green pepper and onion until meat is no longer pink; drain. Stir in the noodles, tomatoes, water, chili sauce, salt and pepper; mix well.

Cover and cook over low heat for 15-20 minutes or until the noodles are tender, stirring frequently. Add bacon. **Yield:** 5 servings.

Sloppy Joe Wagon Wheels

(Pictured below)

Lou Ellen McClinton
Jacksonville, North Carolina

Sloppy joe sauce gives a bit of sweetness to prepared spaghetti sauce in this meaty mixture that I serve over pasta wheels. My family and friends like it and don't realize how easy it is to make.

- **1 package (16 ounces) wagon wheel pasta**
- **2 pounds ground beef**
- **1 medium green pepper, chopped**
- **1 medium onion, chopped**
- **1 jar (28 ounces) meatless spaghetti sauce**
- **1 jar (15-1/2 ounces) sloppy joe sauce**

Cook pasta according to package directions. Meanwhile, in a large skillet, cook beef, green pepper and onion until meat is no longer pink; drain. Stir in the spaghetti sauce and sloppy joe sauce; heat through. Drain pasta; top with beef mixture. **Yield:** 8 servings.

Pasta Carbonara

Cathy Lorenzini, St. Charles, Missouri

This rich pasta toss is great for everyday dinners or special occasions. I can come home from work and throw this dish together in a half hour. Wherever I take it, I'm constantly asked for the recipe.

- **3 cups uncooked tube pasta**
- **6 bacon strips, diced**
- **2 garlic cloves, minced**
- **1-1/4 cups milk**
- **1 package (8 ounces) cream cheese, cubed**
- **1/2 cup butter, cubed**
- **1/2 cup grated Parmesan cheese**

Cook pasta according to package directions. Meanwhile, in a large skillet, cook bacon until crisp. Remove to paper towels.

In the drippings, saute garlic until tender. Add the milk, cream cheese and butter; stir until smooth. Stir in the Parmesan cheese and bacon; heat through. Drain pasta; toss with sauce. **Yield:** 4 servings.

Hurry-Up Ham 'n' Noodles

Lucille Howell, Portland, Oregon

This basic hearty dish is ready to serve in almost the time it takes to cook the noodles. It is super for a luncheon or any time I'm in a hurry.

- **5 to 6 cups uncooked wide egg noodles**
- **1/4 cup butter**
- **1 cup heavy whipping cream**
- **1-1/2 cups julienned fully cooked ham**
- **1/2 cup grated Parmesan cheese**
- **1/4 cup thinly sliced green onions**
- **1/4 teaspoon salt**
- **1/8 teaspoon pepper**

Cook noodles according to package directions. Meanwhile, in a skillet over medium heat, melt butter. Stir in cream. Bring to a boil; cook and stir for 2 minutes.

Add ham, cheese, onions, salt and pepper;

heat through. Drain noodles; add to ham mixture and heat through. **Yield:** 4 servings.

Hamburger Macaroni Skillet

(Pictured on page 98)

Teresa Ray, Lewisburg, Tennessee

This flavorful meal is great for busy nights because it's a snap to prepare. While leftovers freeze well, there's usually nothing left!

1-1/2 pounds ground beef
1-1/2 to 2 teaspoons garlic powder
2 cups uncooked elbow macaroni
2 cans (10-3/4 ounces *each*) condensed tomato with roasted garlic and herbs soup, undiluted
1-3/4 cups water
2 cups frozen mixed vegetables

In a large skillet, cook beef and garlic powder over medium heat until meat is no longer pink; drain. Stir in the macaroni, soup, water and vegetables. Bring to a boil. Reduce heat; simmer, uncovered, for 20 minutes or until macaroni is tender. **Yield:** 6-8 servings.

Pineapple Chicken Lo Mein

(Pictured above right)

Linda Stevens, Madison, Alabama

The perfect supper to serve on weeknights, this speedy lo mein combines tender chicken and colorful veggies with a tangy sauce. Quick-cooking spaghetti and canned pineapple make it a cinch to assemble when time is short.

1 can (20 ounces) unsweetened pineapple chunks
1 pound boneless skinless chicken breasts, cut into 1-inch cubes

2 garlic cloves, minced
3/4 teaspoon ground ginger *or* 1 tablespoon minced fresh gingerroot
3 tablespoons vegetable oil, *divided*
2 medium carrots, julienned
1 medium green pepper, julienned
4 ounces spaghetti, cooked and drained
3 green onions, sliced
1 tablespoon cornstarch
1/3 cup soy sauce

Drain pineapple, reserving 1/3 cup juice (discard remaining juice or save for another use); set pineapple aside.

In a large skillet over medium heat, cook the chicken, garlic and ginger in 2 tablespoons oil for 6 minutes. Add the carrots, green pepper and pineapple. Cover and cook for 2-3 minutes or until vegetables are crisp-tender and chicken juices run clear. Stir in spaghetti and onions.

In a small bowl, combine the cornstarch, soy sauce, reserved pineapple juice and remaining oil until smooth. Stir into chicken mixture. Bring to a boil; cook and stir for 2 minutes or until thickened. **Yield:** 4 servings.

Bean and Ham Pasta

(Pictured above)

Maureen De Garmo, Concord, California

I often assemble this pleasant pasta medley that's brimming with ham, corn and black beans. If you'd like, you can thicken the juices with cornstarch to make a sauce. Either way, it's delicious.

- **1 can (14-1/2 ounces) chicken broth**
- **1-1/2 cups uncooked spiral pasta**
- **1 can (15 ounces) black beans, rinsed and drained**
- **1-1/2 cups frozen corn**
- **1 cup cubed fully cooked ham**
- **1/4 teaspoon dried thyme**
- **Salt and pepper to taste**
- **Dash ground cumin**
- **1/4 cup shredded Parmesan cheese**

In a large saucepan, bring broth to a boil. Add the pasta; cook, uncovered, for 10 minutes or until tender. Do not drain.

Stir in the beans, corn, ham and seasonings; heat through. Sprinkle with cheese. **Yield:** 4 servings.

Seafood Alfredo

Melissa Mosness, Loveland, Colorado

This rich, creamy main dish features plenty of seafood flavors with a hint of garlic and lemon. Frozen peas and a jar of Alfredo sauce make it a simple supper that will be requested time and again.

- **1 package (12 ounces) bow tie pasta**
- **2 garlic cloves, minced**
- **2 tablespoons olive oil**
- **1 package (8 ounces) imitation crabmeat, flaked**
- **1 package (5 ounces) frozen cooked salad shrimp, thawed**
- **1 tablespoon lemon juice**
- **1/2 teaspoon pepper**
- **1 jar (16 ounces) Alfredo sauce**
- **1/2 cup frozen peas, thawed**
- **1/4 cup shredded Parmesan cheese**

Cook pasta according to package directions. Meanwhile, in a large skillet, saute garlic in oil until tender. Stir in the crab, shrimp, lemon juice and pepper. Cook and stir for 1 minute.

Add Alfredo sauce and peas. Cook and stir until heated through. Drain pasta; top with the seafood mixture and sprinkle with Parmesan cheese. **Yield:** 4-6 servings.

Curly Noodle Pork Supper

Carmen Carlson, Kent, Washington

This hearty meal-in-one is loaded with tender pork and ramen noodles. Broccoli and red pepper add a bounty of fresh-from-the-garden flavor that will bring 'em back for seconds.

- **1 pound pork tenderloin, cut into 1/4-inch strips**

- 1 medium sweet red pepper, cut into 1-inch pieces
- 1 cup broccoli florets
- 4 green onions, cut into 1-inch pieces
- 1 tablespoon vegetable oil
- 1-1/2 cups water
- 2 packages (3 ounces *each*) pork ramen noodles
- 1 tablespoon minced fresh parsley
- 1 tablespoon soy sauce

In a large skillet, cook pork, red pepper, broccoli and onions in oil until meat is no longer pink. Add the water, noodles with contents of seasoning packets, parsley and soy sauce. Bring to a boil. Reduce heat; cook for 3-4 minutes or until noodles are tender. **Yield:** 3-4 servings.

Spicy Pepper Penne

Candace Greene, Columbiana, Ohio

I sure know how to bring a bit of Sicily to the supper table! Let my zesty combination of pepperoni, pasta and peppers add a little kick to your dinner lineup.

- 1 package (16 ounces) penne *or* tube pasta
- 1/2 teaspoon minced fresh rosemary *or* 1/8 teaspoon dried rosemary, crushed
- 2 packages (3-1/2 ounces *each*) sliced pepperoni, halved
- 1/2 cup sliced pepperoncinis
- 1 jar (7 ounces) roasted sweet red peppers, drained and chopped
- 3-1/2 cups boiling water
- 1/2 cup heavy whipping cream
- 1/2 cup grated Parmesan cheese

In a large skillet, layer the pasta, rosemary, pepperoni, pepperoncinis and red peppers. Add water; bring to a boil. Reduce heat; cover and simmer for 12 minutes or until pasta is tender. Add cream and Parmesan cheese; toss to coat. **Yield:** 8 servings.

Editor's Note: Look for pepperoncinis (pickled peppers) in the pickle and olive section of your grocery store.

Ravioli Primavera

(Pictured below)

Lois McAtee, Oceanside, California

I rely on frozen vegetables and ravioli to hurry along this colorful main dish. It's pleasantly seasoned with minced garlic and fresh parsley.

- 4 cups frozen miniature cheese ravioli
- 1 package (16 ounces) frozen Italian vegetables, thawed
- 2 garlic cloves, minced
- 1/4 cup olive oil
- 1/4 cup chicken *or* vegetable broth
- 2 tablespoons minced fresh parsley
- 1/4 teaspoon salt
- 1/4 teaspoon pepper

Prepare ravioli according to package directions. Meanwhile, in a large skillet, saute vegetables and garlic in oil for 4 minutes. Stir in the broth. Simmer, uncovered, for 2 minutes.

Stir in the parsley, salt and pepper; cook 2 minutes longer or until vegetables are tender. Drain pasta; add to vegetable mixture and toss to coat. **Yield:** 4 servings.

Garlic Shrimp Pasta

(Pictured below)

Amy Varner, Rio Rancho, New Mexico

This recipe is elegant, yet it doesn't require hours of working in the kitchen. Everyone agrees it's quite a treat.

4 garlic cloves, minced
1/3 cup butter
3/4 cup heavy whipping cream
1/4 cup minced fresh parsley
1 teaspoon minced fresh dill *or* 1/4 teaspoon dill weed
1/4 teaspoon salt
Dash pepper
1/2 pound uncooked medium shrimp, peeled and deveined
3 ounces thin spaghetti *or* angel hair pasta, cooked and drained

In a small skillet, cook garlic in butter for 1 minute. Whisk in cream, parsley, dill, salt and pepper. Bring to a boil. Reduce heat; simmer, uncovered, for about 13 minutes or until sauce is thickened, stirring occasionally. Add shrimp to pan. Cook and stir for about 2 minutes or until shrimp turn pink. Pour over pasta; toss to coat. Serve immediately. **Yield:** 2 servings.

Pretty Ham Primavera

Joan Laurenzo, Johnstown, Ohio

I give my leftover ham a face-lift in this tasty pasta dish. The mild cream sauce gets fresh flavor from sauteed mushrooms and color from peas.

1/2 pound fresh mushrooms, sliced
1 small onion, chopped
2 tablespoons olive oil
2 tablespoons all-purpose flour
2 teaspoons Italian seasoning
2 teaspoons chicken bouillon granules
1/2 teaspoon salt
1/8 teaspoon pepper
2 cups milk
1 package (7 ounces) thin spaghetti, cooked and drained
2 cups cubed fully cooked ham (1 pound)
1 package (10 ounces) frozen peas, thawed
Grated Parmesan cheese

In a large skillet, saute mushrooms and onion in oil until tender. Stir in flour, Italian seasoning, bouillon, salt and pepper until smooth. Gradually add milk, stirring constantly. Bring to a boil; boil and stir for 2 minutes. Stir in the spaghetti, ham and peas; heat through. Sprinkle with Parmesan cheese. **Yield:** 4 servings.

Meatballs Monte Carlo

Margaret Wilson, Hemet, California

I need just one pan to prepare this easy entree. Once the meatballs have browned, the egg noodles cook in the sauce.

1/3 cup evaporated milk
1/4 cup dry bread crumbs
1 small onion, chopped
1/4 teaspoon salt
Dash pepper
1 pound ground beef
1 envelope spaghetti sauce mix

- 4 cans (11-1/2 ounces *each*) tomato juice
- 1 cup water
- 5 cups uncooked extra wide egg noodles
- 1 can (2-1/4 ounces) sliced ripe olives, drained

In a large bowl, combine milk, bread crumbs, onion, salt and pepper. Crumble beef over mixture and mix well. Shape into 1-1/2-in. balls.

In a large skillet over medium-high heat, brown meatballs; drain. Combine the spaghetti sauce mix, tomato juice and water; pour over the meatballs. Bring to a boil. Stir in the noodles and olives. Reduce heat; cover and simmer for 20-25 minutes or until noodles are tender, stirring occasionally. **Yield:** 6 servings.

Pork Lo Mein

(Pictured at right)

Linda Trainor, Phoenix, Arizona

This full-flavored stir-fry is sure to bring rave reviews from your family. Snappy snow peas, sweet pepper and pork are spiced up with ginger, sesame oil, red pepper flakes and soy sauce.

- 1 pork tenderloin (1 pound)
- 1/4 cup soy sauce
- 3 garlic cloves, minced
- 1/4 teaspoon ground ginger *or* 1 teaspoon minced fresh gingerroot
- 1/4 teaspoon crushed red pepper flakes
- 2 cups fresh snow peas
- 1 medium sweet red pepper, julienned
- 3 cups cooked thin spaghetti
- 1/3 cup chicken broth
- 2 teaspoons sesame oil

Cut tenderloin in half lengthwise. Cut each half widthwise into 1/4-in. slices; set aside. In a large resealable plastic bag, combine the soy sauce, garlic, ginger and pepper flakes; add pork. Seal bag and turn to coat; refrigerate for 20 minutes.

In a large nonstick skillet or wok coated with nonstick cooking spray, stir-fry pork and marinade for 4-5 minutes or until meat is no longer pink. Add peas and red pepper; stir-fry for 1 minute. Stir in spaghetti and broth; cook 1 minute longer. Remove from the heat; stir in sesame oil. **Yield:** 4 servings.

Italian Noodles

Barbara Thomas, Mankato, Kansas

I seldom know if I'm going to have one, two or 15 people at the table for meals, so I need fast, simple recipes. This one's both—plus tasty.

- 4 cups uncooked egg noodles
- 1/2 pound ground beef
- 1/4 pound miniature smoked sausage links
- 2 cups frozen corn, thawed
- 1 jar (26 ounces) spaghetti sauce
- 1 cup (8 ounces) small-curd cottage cheese
- 1/4 teaspoon garlic powder
- 1/2 cup shredded mozzarella cheese

Cook noodles according to package directions. Meanwhile, in a large skillet, cook beef and sausage over medium heat until beef is no longer pink; drain. Add corn, spaghetti sauce, cottage cheese and garlic powder; heat through. Drain noodles; stir into beef mixture. Sprinkle with cheese. Cover and cook for 5 minutes or until cheese melts. **Yield:** 4-6 servings.

General Recipe Index

This index lists every recipe by major ingredient(s).